shine

Be an excellent employee, take control
of your career and fulfil your potential

Jenny Ungless

Shine: Be an excellent employee, take control of your career and fulfil your potential

This edition first published in 2011 by Trotman Publishing, a division of Crimson Publishing Ltd, Westminster House, Kew Road, Richmond, Surrey TW9 2ND

© Trotman Publishing 2011

Author: Jenny Ungless

British Library Cataloguing in Publication Data
A catalogue record for this book is available from the British Library

ISBN: 978 1 84455 377 8

Typeset by RefineCatch Ltd, Bungay Suffolk
Printed and bound in Great Britain by TJ International, Padstow, Cornwall

Contents

About the author

Jenny Ungless is one of the UK's top career coaches. Following 10 years in the political world, Jenny set up City Life Coaching, which is now a leading provider of career coaching to young professionals. Jenny is also the career guru for Monster, the UK and Ireland's top online recruitment site.

Jenny's advice on careers is regularly featured in national newspapers including the *Guardian*, *The Times* and the *Independent*, as well as a range of other magazines and publications. Jenny's first book, *Career Ahead: The complete career handbook*, was published by Raleo Publishing in December 2008.

Jenny is also a Director of Watson Helsby, a leading specialist executive search firm.

Jenny lives in London with her husband, James.

Introduction: why you need to shine

This book is all about how to excel at work. But why do you need to 'shine'? Because we live in a world where 'good enough' doesn't cut it any more. Developments in technology and the growth of emerging markets mean that more and more jobs are being outsourced: there's always someone who can do it more cheaply than you. The recent financial crisis has had – and will continue to have – a devastating impact on jobs in both the public and private sectors. People who thought they had a job for life are finding themselves facing redundancy. The pressure is on organisations of every shape and size to do things more efficiently, more cheaply, better.

In circumstances like this, there's no room for complacency. The people who simply turn up and do a good enough job are the ones who will be shown the door. Only the best will survive. Sometimes even the best don't survive. If you're not one of the best, you've got no chance!

But it's not just about being the excellent employee who hangs on to their job when times are tough. Being someone who shines at work puts you in control of your career. If you know how to play to your strengths, how to portray your personal brand, how to lead, influence and manage, how to be creative and build connections, people will come knocking on your door. By giving your very best at whatever you do, you will open up a whole range of opportunities for yourself. Other people will want you on board.

Last – but definitely not least – you owe it to yourself to be the best that you can be, to fulfil your potential. You owe it to yourself to find work that is challenging, satisfying and fun. You owe it to yourself to be excellent at what you do. In short, you owe it to yourself to shine.

PART

1

DISCOVERING WHAT YOU WANT

To excel at work you need to be in a job that is right for you. That means finding a working environment that suits your values, a role which plays to your skills and strengths, and one that genuinely interests you. If you're not truly engaged with what you do every day, you'll find it very hard – if not impossible – to shine. So the starting point in building a stellar career for yourself is self-awareness: knowing what really makes you tick.

1

Establish your motivations

The key to building a career where you can really shine is to know what your work means to you. We all have different motivations for working, apart from merely having to earn a living. Being clear about your work 'motivators' is the starting point for developing a career that really suits you – and where you can excel.

Why we work

Work is an important part of most people's lives. Why? Well, to put it bluntly, most of us need to work to earn a living! Money is also a key element of the reward we get for the work that we do – and it's often the most tangible form of recognition. That said, research shows that money is a 'hygiene' factor: in other words, if we feel that we are being paid a fair rate for the work we do, then money itself is not a key motivator for most people. Other factors, such as praise and verbal recognition, team spirit and a feeling of being included, tend to be more important.

Clearly, though, your salary expectations will have a strong influence on the career decisions that you make. So it's good to think about how much money you really need. Everyone has to make their own trade-offs, and only you can decide the degree of financial sacrifice that you are prepared to make in order to do something that you really enjoy. It may be an uncomfortable issue to wrestle with, but it's not something you should hide your head in the sand over.

It's not just about money

If financial gain was all that was important, it wouldn't really matter what job you did, as long as it paid the bills. Apart from financial reward, what else can we derive from our work?

Firstly, work can give us a sense of identity and status. When you meet someone new, the first question you usually ask them is (after their name): 'What do you do?'. Our work helps to define us. Other people will make assumptions about our personality, our intellect or our lifestyle based on the work that we do. When I work with clients who are looking to change career direction, one of the things they often tell me is that they are embarrassed to tell people what they do for a living. That's a clear sign that their work is not a good fit for them. Conversely, people who love their jobs often love to talk about what they do – it's meaningful to them and they are proud of their profession.

Work also gives us a structure for our lives. While we've all had daydreams about never having to work again, most of us actually benefit from the structure and discipline that a job gives us. Work can also give us a sense of achievement, fulfilment and identity that it's hard to derive from other sources.

Depending on what we do, work can also be fun! Fun at work usually comes from the people that we work with, rather than the tasks that we do. Work gives us a chance to interact and connect with others, to meet new people and make friends. How many of your friends have you met through work? And a large proportion of us meet our partners through work too: it's one of the best dating agencies there is!

MAKING IT WORK IN PRACTICE

Finding your work motivation

Take 10 minutes to sit down with a notebook and think about your personal motivations for working: aim to identify your top five, in order of priority. These might include:

- *a certain level of income to allow you to support yourself, your family and your lifestyle choices*

- *work that is meaningful to you and that you can be proud of*

- *a high level of autonomy and independence in what you do*

- *opportunities to continue learning and developing*

- *the social support that comes from being part of an organisation and working with like-minded people.*

These options aren't mutually exclusive: some or all of them might be important to you in varying degrees. But being as precise as you can about what you want to derive from your professional life is the starting point for finding a role where you can excel. If you're not getting what you want from work, you'll find it very hard to stay motivated and engaged.

Work: a job, a career or a vocation?

Now that you have identified your motivations you should be clearer about what you really want to get from your work. However, it's also worth thinking about how you see your work fitting into the rest of your life. For some people, work is simply a job: something that puts food on the table and allows you to pursue your interests outside of work. Other people think of their work in terms of a career: a path where they can progress and get promoted, for example, or as a way of continuing to develop professionally and personally. And, for some people, their career is a 'calling': something that gives their lives purpose and meaning and which they feel is their vocation.

This last point is something which, over my years working as a career coach, I have seen more and more often. Many of the clients who come to me for careers advice are successful young professionals – lawyers, bankers, management consultants, for example – who earn good salaries and have a clear structure for the progression of their career. So why do they come to me? Time and again clients say to me that they feel there is 'something missing' from their work life, that they want to do something that is more 'fulfilling' or that has a greater sense of purpose. Increasingly, it seems, we want work that truly motivates and inspires us.

It's also important to realise that your work, whether it is a job, a career or a vocation, has very little, if anything, to do with the nature of the work you do. It's all about how *you* perceive it. It's easy to fall into the trap of thinking that a 'job' is something menial, while a 'career' is a role where you have a defined structure for progression and promotion, and a vocation is the kind of term we might associate with doctors or vicars, but it really is much more about your mindset than about the nature of what you do. It's about what your work means to you.

So, how do you identify whether you want your work to be simply a job, or a career, or a vocation? For starters, think about how you see your work fitting into your lifestyle. If work–life balance is important to you, for example, and you want to be able to leave the office at the end of the day, close the door behind you and get on with the rest of your life, then you're probably looking for a role that you can regard as simply a job. If you would like to see yourself progressing up the ladder, taking on more responsibility and gaining more status, then I would describe that as a career. And, if you have a burning passion to make a difference – at whatever level – then you might describe that as a vocation. Whichever of these applies to you, this book is relevant: whether you look on work as a job, a career or a vocation, you owe it to yourself to enjoy what you do and to do it well.

REAL LIFE

My client Carol was very clear that she was looking for a fulfilling and interesting job, but not a career or a vocation. She didn't want to 'move up the ladder' and take on increasing levels of responsibility. She didn't have any huge desire to make the world a better place. She simply wanted a role that interested her, that she could do well and that would give her the means – but also the time – to indulge in her hobbies and other interests. She ended up taking on a position as PA to the head of a university department. It's a job where she uses her key skills of problem-solving, administration and people management, but where she doesn't have significant levels of responsibility and where – particularly out of term-time – she has plenty of time to do the other things that she enjoys, such as sport and music. For her, it's the perfect role.

IN A NUTSHELL

• Work means different things to each of us. Being clear about what your work motivations are will help you to identify the best opportunities.

• You might see your work as simply a job, as a career or as a vocation. Whatever your outlook, you owe it to yourself to find work that you enjoy.

If you'd like to learn more about finding out what motivates you at work, I recommend:
Nick Williams, *The Work We Were Born to Do*, Element, 2009.

A thoughtful guide to discovering your work motivations and planning your career.

2

Know your values

Successful career planning is about knowing who you are, what you want to get from work and how you want your work to fit into your life and lifestyle. The key to planning – and being successful in – your career is knowing yourself: in particular, your values and expectations. That way you can begin to match your career choice, and the way in which you develop your career, to your own needs and preferences.

How well do you know yourself?

In the last chapter we looked at **why** we work. Now that you have identified these reasons you need to go one step further and think about the **kind** of work that suits you and your motivations best – because doing what you're really good at, and enjoy, is a sure-fire way to shine.

The good news is that the information you need to plan your career effectively is, for the most part, information that you already have. You might need to articulate your thoughts and feelings a bit more clearly, but most of us know deep down what is important to us. We know the kinds of task that we enjoy and are good at, and the subjects and issues that interest us. And these are the key elements of successful career planning.

I use a simple equation with my career coaching clients:

VALUES + INTERESTS + PREFERRED (SKILLS + WORKING STYLE)

=

THE RIGHT CAREER!

This is a simple shorthand way of defining the key elements of successful career planning. In this chapter, we'll look more closely at your values and how they should inform your career choices. In the following chapters, we'll look at how to use your skills, working style and interests to help you identify the kinds of role where you'll be most fulfilled.

Your values and expectations

The basis for a good career plan – and a good life plan – is knowing what is important to you: your values. While most of us know what matters to us and what 'makes us tick' sometimes we can find it a bit hard to articulate this: it's not something we're really used to talking about, especially in the context of work. But it's critical in terms of your career management and success that you clearly outline what values matter most to you. Thinking about your values will help you to identify the kind of working environment that you will most enjoy, the sorts of role that will suit you best and the types of industry sector and organisation where you are most likely to find fulfilment. Not only will it help you to make good career choices, it will also help you to make lifestyle choices that are right for you, and get the balance right between work and other aspects of your life.

When I talk about 'values', my definition is pretty broad. You might think of values as things like integrity, honesty or morality – and of course these kinds of ethical values are very important. But I would encourage you to define your 'values' as 'the things that you value' or 'the things that are important to you'. In a work context, that means that values can encompass issues such as independence, power, status, as well as much more practical things such as your salary and working environment. We'll see below how values can be both 'extrinsic' and 'intrinsic'.

Imagine being in a job where you love the people you work with, you're proud of the company you work for and where you know that the work you do is recognised and appreciated. Sounds good, doesn't it? This is the kind of scenario you can expect if your employer and your colleagues share your values.

REAL LIFE

One of my clients, Karen, recently came to me for help because she found a conflict of values in her current role. She works in a marketing role, which she really enjoys, but she describes the culture of the company as 'hard' and 'cold'. It's too profit-focused for her, so she is looking to transfer her skills into an environment where people really care about each other and about their customers. The fact that Karen has recognised that she has found a role that suits her but not an environment that suits her values means she can begin to look for a role in a company which does match her values.

If, on the other hand, you find yourself in a workplace that doesn't match your values, you're going to struggle to enjoy your work. It's hard to be happy – or successful – in an environment where the company culture doesn't suit you, where the aspects of work that are most important to you are not the ones that are rewarded or where you simply don't have anything in common with your work colleagues.

> **TIP**
>
> *Your values are a very useful tool to help you distinguish between different employers, even ones within the same industry sector. Organisations and companies all have their own culture and ways of working, and you need to identify the ones whose values and ethos match your own. That way you will be a round peg in a round hole, not a round peg in a square hole.*

Intrinsic and extrinsic values

Values can be divided into two broad categories: intrinsic and extrinsic. *Intrinsic* values (essentially internal factors such as how you relate to the world and other people) can include your level of integrity, the importance you attach to building strong relationships or the degree of independence or security you need from the work that you do. *Extrinsic* values on the other hand are essentially your attitude to external factors such as your working environment or salary. Both are important: if your work situation doesn't allow you to live in accordance with your intrinsic values, you're likely to feel uncomfortable because you are compromising on your personal standards and style. Similarly, if your extrinsic values aren't being met, you're likely to feel dissatisfied and possibly even resentful about your work.

Intrinsic values

First of all, let's look at your intrinsic values. These are the factors that are fundamentally important to you as an individual, and that define your character and personality.

MAKING IT WORK IN PRACTICE

Identifying your core intrinsic values
Take 20 minutes to make a list of your core intrinsic values. Here are
some questions to get you thinking.

- *Is it important for you to feel a **connection** with your work –*
  does it need to be something that really 'matters' to you?

- *Do you want to nourish your **creativity**, for example by being*
  encouraged to come up with, and implement, new ideas?

- *Do you need a feeling of **freedom**, for example through being*
  able to take ownership of your work?

- *Do you need a sense of **security** – for instance, how important*
  is it for you to work in a stable environment where lay-offs and
  redundancies are unlikely?

- *Do you need a high degree of **independence** – do you like to be*
  left to 'get on with things'?

- *How important is **quality** to you – for example, do you like to be*
  in an environment where it's standard to 'go the extra mile'?

- *Do you need to feel **recognition** – how important is it to you*
  that your colleagues and managers regularly acknowledge and
  praise your efforts?

- *Do you want to achieve a **balance** between life and work – are*
  you happy to work long hours, or do you want to be able to
  leave work behind at the end of day and concentrate on other
  things?

- *Is it important for you to feel you have **power** in what you do –*
  for example, do you relish the authority to take decisions, or do
  you prefer other people to assume responsibility?

Of course this isn't an exhaustive list: make your own list as
comprehensive as possible. Start with a list of words that represent what
really matters to you, for example: status, security, relationships and

so on. Then try to define exactly what each of these means to you. For example, if you've chosen 'security', what precisely do you mean by that? What's your definition of security? It could be financial, emotional, physical or a blend of these. If you've chosen 'creativity', what exactly does that mean to you? Perhaps you mean that you'd like a job that involves lots of writing, or maybe what you really mean by a creative role is one where you have to do lots of problem-solving or thinking on your feet. Be as specific as you can about what your values would look like in practice.

Finally, whittle your list down to the four or five factors that best represent the person you are and what you need from your work. Weigh your values against each other to help you decide which are the most important. This isn't an exact science, of course, but use your gut instinct to help you decide which values you might be prepared to compromise on, and which ones are 'non-negotiable'. For example, while recognition from others could be something that matters to you, you might decide that, ultimately, it's more important to you to be able to work autonomously, even if that means that your profile is lower in your workplace. This list of four or five factors are your essential values, the things that you should be seeking to base your lifestyle and career choices on. By the way, no one's saying that the average person has only four values, but being forced to narrow down your choices helps you to focus on your real priorities.

TIP

*Try to be as honest as you can. It's easy to fall into the trap of choosing values that we think we 'ought' to have. But the only values that matter are the ones that matter to **you**.*

Extrinsic values

Now carry out the same 'Making it work in practice' exercise to establish your extrinsic values (which you could also think of as your practical needs or expectations). In other words, take stock of what you really want in physical terms. That could be in relation to salary, location, flexible working arrangements, training and development opportunities. These are all factors that can have a significant impact on your enjoyment of work – and your life outside work. For example, you may have a role that you really enjoy, but if you have a two-hour commute to work each day and end up getting home late and exhausted, you probably haven't got the balance quite right.

REAL LIFE

My client Nigel is a lawyer in a London property firm. While he enjoys his work, he has a young family and he's keen to relocate outside of London. In an ideal world, he'd be able to work close to his new home, but he knows that that will limit his career choices: most top law firms tend to be based in London or other major cities. He's prepared to trade off a longer commute for the gain of having more career progression opportunities, and being able to raise his family in the countryside. Other people in a similar situation – where they want to progress their career but don't enjoy all aspects of city life – might look at different options: for example, staying in town during the week and living in the country at weekends, or negotiating to work a day a week from home so that they don't have a long commute every day. Often there are compromises we can make that help us to get the best – or nearly the best – of both worlds.

In particular, try to get clear about which areas you aren't prepared to compromise on, and those areas where you would be happy to make some kind of trade-off. This is the information you need to use to help you make decisions about what comes next in your career.

IN A NUTSHELL

- Your values should inform and underpin the career choices you make. If you're not working in accordance with your values, you won't be able to shine.

- Know what your values look like in practice: what are your intrinsic and extrinsic values?

- Be clear about what you're prepared to compromise on and what you're not.

If you'd like to learn more about discovering your values, I recommend:
Judith Leary-Joyce, *The Psychology of Success: Secrets of serial achievement*, Pearson Education Ltd, 2009.

Thought-provoking material on identifying your values and needs in a work context.

3

Define your brand

How you 'market' yourself at work, and how other people perceive you, is fundamental in helping you to shine. Each of us has our own unique blend of skills and strengths, and our preferred working style. Drawing these together into a description of your personal 'brand' will help you to stand out from the crowd.

The power of brands

In a world where we are bombarded with advertising, we all know the power of brands. Some brands are so famous that their names have actually become synonymous with the product they represent: we talk about doing the 'hoovering', not the 'vacuum cleaning', and 'Google' has become the word most of us use to describe a search on the internet. In much the same way, you need to start to think of your professional persona as a brand. Being clear about what you have to offer is a sure way to shine at work.

The guru of personal branding is the management expert Tom Peters, who, for well over a decade, has been writing about the need for individuals to regard themselves, not as employees or workers, but as the 'CEO' of their own life and career. Managing your career is your responsibility, and yours alone, and the key to success is knowing how and where you can add value in the workplace. Your personal brand is, in Peters' words, your 'promise to the marketplace and the world'.

Put simply, your brand is how you describe yourself to other people. It's your personal package of skills, characteristics and experience. It's about what you represent, and what makes you special. It's the way in which you want the world to see you. In very practical terms, your brand statement should be the starting point for every CV you write, every interview you undertake: indeed, every occasion on which you have to present or talk about yourself. You need to be crystal clear about the two or three points that you want to get across about your professional persona, experience and approach – and how you talk about those.

So how do you go about identifying and articulating your brand? I suggest you focus on three areas:

1. **your skills**

2. **your strengths**

3. **your working style.**

Identify your core skills

Sit down for 20 minutes or so and write a list of your top 10 skills: what kind of tasks are you best at and what are the ones you most enjoy? Divide your skills into three categories:

1. **skills related to people,** eg coaching, communicating, presenting, training, counselling, negotiating, influencing, managing

2. **skills related to information,** eg researching, analysing, problem-solving, organising, editing, innovating, writing, designing

3. **skills related to things,** eg computing, building, creating, fixing, styling, co-ordinating.

How balanced is your list? Is there one category which is much bigger than the others? What are the main themes of your skill set? Is there one set of skills that is dominant? For example, perhaps all of your core skills are people-orientated. That should tell you a lot about the kind of role that you are likely to excel in – probably not one where you are sat in front of a computer screen for eight hours a day!

Compare your skills list with your job description: are there important skills that you are missing? Do you have several core skills that you never get a chance to use in your job? Think about how good a match your current role is for your skill set. Your conclusion might be that you need some training on a couple of areas to broaden out your skills – or it might be that you need to look for a role that makes much better use of the skills that you have. Either way, you need to be aware of how good the 'fit' is between your existing role and your current skills; only then are you in a position to decide what, if any, changes you need to make.

Identify your strengths

As well as your skills, take a few minutes to think about what might be described as your *strengths*. Where skills are things that you have been taught to do (either by yourself or others), think of strengths as your natural characteristics, for example a sense of curiosity, the ability to keep calm in a crisis, a natural rapport with people and so on.

> **TIP**
>
> *This is not a time for false modesty! We all have special skills and talents: make sure you are clear what yours are.*

The eminent psychologist Martin Seligman has identified 24 main strengths, and if you go to his website (www.authentichappiness.org) you can take his strengths test for free. Seligman suggests that we can make our work life more satisfying by identifying and focusing on our key or 'signature' strengths, and my experience has shown that focusing on these strengths really can help you to shine.

Get feedback

Of course, it's not enough for you alone to have an idea of what your brand is, what's critical is how other people perceive you. Whether you like it or not, the people you work with have an opinion about you. They might think you're extrovert, glamorous, ruthless, friendly, geeky etc, the list goes on. To manage your brand effectively you not only need to know yourself, you need to know how other people perceive you – some aspects of which you might want to try to change!

That's why, when you're trying to identify and develop your brand, it's a good idea to get a bit of feedback from other people. Of course you are the person who knows yourself best, but sometimes we underestimate or miss out on skills because we don't think they're anything special or we assume everyone else has them too. These are what are known as your 'hidden skills'. Other people often see qualities in us that we don't. Don't feel shy about asking for feedback: people will understand that you are simply trying to get a better understanding of how you come across.

Select five or six people who know you well – ideally a mixture of friends, family and former or current work colleagues – and ask them the following questions (you can do it by email if it's too embarrassing face to face!).

- What are the first five words you think of when you think of me?

- What would you say are my top five skills?

- What would you turn to me for advice about/help with?

- What makes me special?

What are the consistent points in the feedback you receive? Different people will use different words to describe much the same thing, so it's better to think in terms of themes rather than specific words. For example, one person might say that you are good at prioritising, someone else might say well-organised and yet another person might describe you as efficient. They are all describing the same broad skill set of personal management.

Think about how well the feedback matches your own description of your skills. Are there any discrepancies? Why might that be? In particular, look out for those hidden skills: what do other people see in you that you have missed?

REAL LIFE

When my client Sophie did this exercise, she was quite surprised at some of the feedback she received. Several of her friends and colleagues highlighted her coaching and mentoring skills – they thought she was great at helping people to think differently about situations, and encouraging them to find their own answers to problems. Sophie worked as an IT trainer for a large retail company, so her job mostly involved teaching staff about new processes and passing on information. Encouraged by her friends' feedback, she eventually moved into a wider training role supporting new graduate trainees, where she was able to make much more use of her mentoring skills.

Your working style

As well as your skills, it's also useful to think about your preferred working style – that is how you like to do things. Are you someone who likes to work autonomously, for instance, or do you prefer to be part of a team and work collaboratively? Perhaps you're someone who likes to be quite sociable and informal at work; alternatively, you might prefer a more structured and professional atmosphere. It's important to think about these things as you're going to do your best work, and be most successful, in an environment that suits you and your working style and where you can be, well, *you*.

MAKING IT WORK IN PRACTICE

Your brand

Set aside half an hour, sit down with a pen and paper, and draft a two or three sentence summary about yourself. This should incorporate your values (as you identified earlier, see pp. 13–14), your key skills and your main attributes. Think of it as your 'elevator pitch': if you met someone in a lift and had only 30 seconds to describe yourself to them, what would you say so that they could get as clear a picture as possible of who you are and what you are like?

Remember, your brand statement is the starting point for every CV you will write (it should form the basis of the 'personal profile' section of your CV), every job application you make (your cover letter needs to set out what makes you special) and every interview you attend (you need to be able to talk about yourself compellingly and convincingly). It's also your template for how you behave at work and the way in which you want other people to think, and talk, about you. So it's worth spending time on it.

Help! I don't like my brand!

What happens if you look at your brand statement – your key skills and strengths – and you don't like what you see? Or what if the feedback you get from other people isn't what you wanted or expected? The good news about your brand is that you can change it. Perhaps you think you need to sharpen up some of your skills – networking, presenting, writing, for example – or you need to raise your game to become more organised, more decisive or a better team player. Think about the brand you'd really like to have – what changes do you need to make? I'm not suggesting that you try completely to reinvent yourself, but if you have identified one or two skills that you'd like to acquire or behaviours that you'd like to change, then these are key areas for you to focus on.

Living your brand

Of course, you not only have to describe your brand, you have to live it! As any marketing guru will tell you, a strong brand is about delivering a clear and consistent message. So, for example, if you want to be seen as someone who is dynamic and positive you need to live that way every day. If you want to be seen as the consummate professional, your clothes, tone and body language need to convey that message. Everything from your personal appearance to your online presence on sites such as LinkedIn and Facebook need to reflect the type of person you want to be seen as.

The work involved in defining – and maintaining – your brand may seem daunting, but it's a critical element of your career planning

REAL LIFE

My friend David is a corporate communications professional, specialising in crisis management. That's his key skill set, but there's much more to his brand than that. David is a brilliant manager, a great networker and the life and soul of any party. He's never seen in a grumpy mood or having a bad day; he's the person that everyone in his team – and beyond – turns to when they need a bit of a boost or some moral support.

It's this blend of skills and personal style that sets David apart and makes his 'brand'.

process. It's key to helping you to sell yourself effectively, and showing your employer what you have to offer. Being clear about your brand will enable you to build your reputation in the professional world, help you to identify good opportunities and give you a benchmark against which to measure your performance.

IN A NUTSHELL

- Defining your brand means knowing what sets you apart and makes you special.

- Each of us has our own unique blend of skills, strengths and personal qualities. Being clear about your best attributes will help you to identify the opportunities and occasions where you can shine.

- If there are elements of your 'brand' that you don't like, the good news is you can change them!

- Once you have identified your brand you need to ensure you live up to that brand, embodying your special skills and strengths in every single aspect of your life.

If you'd like to learn more about defining your brand, I recommend: Tom Peters, *The Brand You 50: Fifty ways to transform yourself from an 'employee' into a brand that shouts distinction, commitment and passion!*, Alfred A. Knopf, 2000.

Although a decade old, this classic publication from the guru of branding is still as relevant – and inspiring – as ever.

Carve out a niche

Being good, or even brilliant, at your job isn't enough if you really want to shine at work. People expect you to be good at your job but if you can find a niche for yourself – a way in which you can add value and make other people's lives easier – you can increase your visibility and build your reputation as a star at work.

The value of a niche

In the last chapter, we looked at how to define and develop your brand – the way people perceive you at work. Another great way of getting yourself noticed at work is to carve out a special niche for yourself.

What do I mean by carving out a niche? I mean finding an area where you can become expert, and that really adds value to your company, your organisation and the work of your colleagues. It's about finding a way in which you can contribute to the company's success, over and above your specific job description. This last point is an important one: as we saw in the previous chapter, if you want to add value to your brand, you need to broaden the extent of your reach within the workplace, and one way of doing that can be to carve out your own niche. So your niche should be something that is relevant across the board, not just to your own area of the business or your own particular role. It's about asking yourself 'What else can I offer that is of value?'

I'll give you a very simple example of what I mean. I'm someone who has always been good at grammar and spelling: some people would no doubt call me a pedant! In many of the roles I've worked in over the years, I've built up a reputation as the person to ask, to check what the appropriate word to use would be, or where an apostrophe should be placed or what the correct spelling of commonly misused words should be in a particular context. It might not seem like a very exciting skill, but in an environment where written material is being put in front of potential customers (whether it's an advertisement, a mail shot or content on a website) first impressions matter, and misspelled words or ungrammatical sentences simply look sloppy. I benefited from being asked to proofread colleagues' work as I was able to build up a reputation as the 'grammar guru' – and even senior colleagues would often double-check their material with me. It was an easy way for me to add extra value to the company, and one that made a real difference to the quality of its output.

The benefits of developing a niche

There are several benefits to developing your own niche, and we'll look at a few of them now.

Getting noticed

Firstly, developing a niche helps you get noticed by more – and often more senior – people. Everyone expects you to be able to do your own job well. But often the only people who really see what you achieve on a day-to-day basis are your immediate colleagues and your boss. And while they will probably notice if you are doing a good job (and will certainly notice if you don't!), that's unlikely to be enough to make them talk about you in glowing terms and help you build your reputation as a superstar. You're expected to be able to do your job – that's what you're paid for, after all.

But if you can find a way of adding value in the workplace which is over and above your job description, people are more likely to notice – and remember, your niche and brand, especially if the expertise you can offer makes their own job easier.

Gaining knowledge

Developing a niche can also be a great way of increasing not just your visibility, but also your knowledge of the business. It can give you an excuse to meet more people, find out about areas of the industry or company other than your own and keep you 'in the loop'. It can help to make you indispensable – and in an uncertain marketplace that can only be a good thing!

Identifying your niche

What are the sorts of skills and expertise that your colleagues will truly value, and where you could carve out a really useful niche? Think about some of the following:

- **proofreading and editing skills**

- **technology skills:** of course big companies have their own IT support gurus, but if you're the person who can sort out the photocopier when it goes on the blink, or who knows how to convert a document into PDF, you're going to be in demand

- **a good memory for names, dates and detail:** being the person in the team who can remember nuggets of information will make you the first port of call when someone else has forgotten something

- **mentoring skills:** being the person who helps new recruits settle in quickly and feel part of the team

- **social skills:** perhaps you could build a reputation as the person who's great at getting people together and encouraging them to socialise.

None of these skills might seem very 'sexy', but they are all ways in which you can help to make a name for yourself as someone who is an extra-useful member of the team.

Carving out an extra niche for yourself will also stand you in good stead as your career progresses. Think of it as having a second string to your bow: you bring value to your organisation in more ways than one.

REAL LIFE

My client Ruthie is an account director with a large public relations firm. While the majority of her time is spent managing her client accounts, she has found the time to develop her interest and expertise in knowledge and talent management. The company where she works has grown very quickly over a relatively short period of time and Ruthie was quick to recognise the challenges this would present in terms of recruiting and retaining good staff, and making sure that people within the organisation continued to share information rather than getting locked into their own managing director and volunteered to put together a presentation on how to manage these challenges. It didn't surprise me at all when, last year, Ruthie was promoted to the company's board: not just because she had shown her commitment to the firm, but because she had identified an area of expertise that she could develop which would be of immense value to the company.

How do you find your niche?

What are the secrets to carving out a successful niche? I think there are three main secrets.

1. **Make sure it's something that other people will value**. Not exactly rocket science, but you're not going to get a lot of credit or exposure for your encyclopaedic knowledge of James Bond movies. (Well, probably not.)

2. **Keep it focused.** You might have heard of the 'Zulu principle' which states that anyone can quickly become an expert in their niche if the niche is small enough. You're not trying to be all things to all people, you're trying to find one way in which you can be useful to lots of people.

3. **Make sure it's something that you are really interested in**. Make your niche something that you already know a lot about, or that you would love to learn more about. Otherwise it will become yet another chore, instead of a way in which you can willingly help other people out.

MAKING IT WORK IN PRACTICE

Advertising your niche

There's not much point in being an expert on something if no one knows about it! So how do you publicise your expertise? You can look for both formal and informal ways of doing this. Formal methods might include writing an article for the in-house magazine, giving a presentation at a company away day or running a short training session for colleagues. A less formal way is simply to be aware of opportunities to help others out: that's not about interfering or being a know-it-all, it's simply about noticing when others are struggling with something that you might be able to help them with. The way in which you build up your reputation as an expert will depend to a large extent on what your area of expertise is, but be prepared to think creatively about what value you can add, and how you can add that value.

IN A NUTSHELL

- Carving out a niche for yourself is a great way to raise your profile at work.

- Think about the ways in which you can add value to your team, your department or the whole business.

- A well-chosen niche will give you an extra string to your bow and help to make you indispensable at work.

- Once you've found your niche, make sure people know about it!

Seek out success

The most important career question you can ask yourself is 'what is my definition of success?'. If you don't know what you're aiming for, your journey becomes a bit pointless. The secret to excelling at your work is to know not just what you are doing, but what you are doing it for.

What does 'success' mean to you?

The question may be simple, but sometimes settling on your answer is less so! Throughout our lives, we have all been influenced by things such as parental expectations, peer pressure, envy of other more 'successful' people and society's apparent obsession with money and fame. All of these influences make it hard for us to be really clear – and honest – about what we want to achieve in our lives and careers. But if you want to have a successful career, you absolutely must be clear about how you – and you alone – define and measure 'success'.

It can be difficult to begin working out how to come up with your own definition of success but it's important that you do. Why? Because the answer to this question will affect not only the kind of work you do, but also the way in which you do it – in particular the hours you work, the level of remuneration that you are happy with and the way in which you fit your job into the rest of your lifestyle.

So far in this book, we've looked at why you work, your values, your skills and strengths, and how to define and develop your 'brand'. Now I want you to pull your thinking on all these issues together to help answer this one simple question.

MAKING IT WORK IN PRACTICE

Envisioning your success

This is an exercise that does require a bit of thinking time: but it's time well spent. Take yourself away somewhere quiet for an hour, and jot down what success at work would look like for you. That might be about how much you earn, or the level you would like to get to in your organisation. Perhaps your dream of success is about running your own business, or being able to work flexibly so that you have lots of time to travel. Whatever you think success would look like, write it down. Articulating your vision will help you to focus on the goals to achieve it.

Note that your definition of success has to be exactly that – *yours*. Try to get away from thinking about what you think success 'should' look like, and focus on what you really *want*. Of course, your definition of success needs to be consistent with what the organisation you work for values, and how it operates. But the starting point is to know how *you* will measure success: finding a workplace that shares your approach and values is the next step.

Ignoring traditional definitions of success

It's all too easy to be influenced by other people's definitions of success, and by what society regards as important. In the world we live in, money, status and power all have kudos attached to them. Most people's career ambitions and expectations are based on the traditional model of progression – essentially more pay and more responsibility as we climb the career ladder. And that's a model which is completely legitimate and which works well for many people. But it's not the only way. Success doesn't always have to be about moving 'up'. Success as society tends to define it almost always has a significant cost attached. You work long hours to earn good money, but often that can be at the price of your health, your relationships and your overall happiness. Of course, lots of people work long hours because they enjoy what they do, are passionate and engaged by it. But you can be passionate about your work without it taking over your whole life. You owe it to yourself to find the balance that is right for you.

Success isn't always 'up'

Career 'progress' doesn't have to mean promotion up the ladder to higher and higher levels of responsibility. In fact, what often happens is that people get promoted into roles that don't suit them and that they don't enjoy. In fact, it's such a common phenomenon that it's known as the 'Peter Principle'. This principle states that people get promoted to their level of incompetence. This can happen because management and HR departments find it difficult to think imaginatively about how to reward and motivate their employees other than promotion, or because they fail to realise that just because someone is effective at one level in an organisation, they will not necessarily perform as well at a higher level. Many an organisation has lost talented and enthusiastic employees because they didn't want to move into management, and the company didn't have the resourcefulness or vision to keep them motivated and challenged at their existing level.

Equally, we as individuals can easily fall into the trap of assuming that the only viable and available career path is upwards. But that doesn't have to be the case. For example, you might choose to develop your niche or specialism, which might not result in a formal promotion, but which can still make you increasingly valuable to your organisation. Or you might decide that the right path for you is actually to do a series of completely different kinds of role over the course of your career – moving around rather than up.

REAL LIFE

My friend Simon was a very talented engineer who worked for a leading aerospace manufacturer, designing, building and maintaining aeroplane engines. He loved the technical, hands-on nature of the work, and he was extremely good at it. In fact, he was so good that he quickly got promoted to management level – and he hated it. He didn't want to spend his time managing a team of design engineers, he wanted to work as a design engineer himself! Eventually, when an opportunity for voluntary redundancy came along, he jumped at the chance. Simon now runs his own successful property firm, buying and renovating run-down houses. He's using both his brain and his hands – exactly what he wanted to do at the aerospace company!

Other ways of working

As well as a range of different routes to career progression, nowadays we have more options than ever before about the way in which we work: 9 to 5, five days a week, doesn't work for everyone. Work is the only thing in our lives that we do day in, day out, for eight or more hours a day. What if it didn't have to be like that? It's worth thinking about some different career 'models'.

The good news is that the world of work is changing. Perhaps not as quickly or as dramatically as some business experts had forecast (the management guru Charles Handy, for example, predicted in the late 1980s that, by the beginning of the 21st century, fewer than half of us would be working in 'proper' full-time jobs), but it's still the case that in the 21st century we have more options open to us than ever before in terms of how we organise our working lives. Why not take some time to think a bit more about the working pattern that is best for you, and that fits best with your values and lifestyle choices? Contract working, flexible working, even a 'portfolio' career where you combine two or more different jobs, are all increasingly common and viable ways of making your job work for you.

Your own business

No book on career management would be complete without at least touching on the subject of self-employment. Many of the clients who come to me for career coaching are attracted to the idea of setting up their own business. It's not surprising: if you're feeling fed up and disillusioned with the corporate world, it's a natural progression to think about doing your own thing. It's not a career choice that suits everyone, of course, but the rewards and benefits can be significant. Running your own business gives you the opportunity to spend your time doing something that you are passionate about. It also gives you an enormous amount of control over what you do, how you do it, and how long you spend doing it. And it gives you the opportunity to earn money for yourself, not for someone else!

Lots of people who fancy the idea of setting up their own business are put off by the perception that they're going to end up working 24 hours a day, seven days a week. And there's no point in denying that it can be hard work. But the bottom line is that it's for you to decide what you want to put into – and get out of – your business. Thousands of people make an extremely good living through their own business without ever hitting the dizzy heights of millionaire status. Not every business-owner wants to scale their business up to become a household name or a multinational brand. Some people choose to set up on their own because it gives them benefits other than, or as well as, money: flexibility, freedom or control, for example. It's about lifestyle choice.

Ultimately, the key to your career success is knowing precisely what success means to you, and how you're going to achieve and measure it. It means enjoying the 'journey' of your career, not just looking forward to some distant end point. In practice, that means setting yourself specific goals – which is what we'll look at in the next chapter.

IN A NUTSHELL

- You'll never be able to call yourself 'successful' if you don't know what success looks like for you.

- There is no single route to success: it's different for each of us.

- Success is not always 'up': there are many more ways of being successful than simply climbing the corporate ladder.

If you'd like to learn more about defining success, I recommend:
Robert Holden, *Success Intelligence: Timeless wisdom for a manic society,* Hodder and Stoughton, 2005.

An in-depth but very readable guide to defining what success means for you, and how to achieve it through work.

Know your goals

Successful people know what they want to achieve in the long-term, and they know what they need to do in the medium and short-term to make that happen. In other words, they have goals. Goals give you direction and structure. But goals by themselves don't lead to anything. Ultimately, a goal is only a dream or an aspiration if you don't take action to make it happen.

Planning for your success

Now that you have come up with your 'success manifesto' you can figure out what steps you need to take to achieve your own definition of success: that is, work out what you need to do to achieve your ambitions. This chapter is all about how to set and achieve the goals that will help you realise your ambitions: but if you don't know what those ambitions are, how can you possibly plan to achieve them?

Take some time (you might need lots of time) to really think about where you see your career going. Where do you want to be in five, 10, 20 years' time? You might not have detailed answers to these questions, but you do need to have a broad picture of what you want to achieve, and where you want to end up, professionally. Otherwise your day-to-day work will just feel a bit pointless – and that's no way to shine!

Setting goals

Goals are about focusing on the specific actions you are going to take to make the progress you want to make towards achieving your ambitions. So they need to be specific, they need to be realistic and you need to commit to taking action to make them happen. You've probably come across a common acronym for goal-setting: SMART. Goals should be **S**pecific, **M**easurable, **A**chievable, **R**elevant and **T**imed. In other words, a goal should describe the action you are going to take, when you are going to take it and how you will know when you have achieved it. Otherwise it's not a goal, it's just a vague aspiration.

The renowned personal development writer Stephen Covey talks about 'beginning with the end in mind'. In other words, you need to know where you want to end up, so that you can plan how to get there from the outset. That's why your most important goals – and the starting point for your planning process – are the long-term ones.

Long-term goals

Your long-term goals are the ones that should most closely resemble your vision for success. Where do you want to be in 10, 20, 30 years' time? This isn't about wishing your life away and not enjoying the present. In fact, it's exactly the opposite: it's about having a purpose and an aim for what you do on a day-to-day basis, as well as looking forward to the future.

Although this is a book about excelling at work, your goals shouldn't be limited to career issues. They should encompass every area of your life – your values, your health, your relationships and your finances, as well as your career aspirations.

For example, your long-term goals might be to get promoted to CEO, to get married and raise a family, to move to the country and to retire when you're 55. Whatever stage of your life and career you're at, it's good to look ahead to the future. Now that you have a vision of your future you need to figure out what you need to do now to make it feasible.

Clients sometimes say to me that they are resistant to the idea of writing down a long-term vision or set of goals, in case it restricts their choices later on. Well, it won't. In fact, having a clear sense of where you want to go allows you to make better judgements and decisions about opportunities that unexpectedly come your way. Why? Because you can assess them against your goals and ask yourself the question 'Is this opportunity likely to take me further away from, or closer to, where I want to be?' Most of us, at some time in our life, will have taken a career decision simply because an opportunity presented itself – someone offered you a job, or a head-hunter called out of the blue. And often we look back and realise that, although we leapt at the offer at the time, in hindsight it wasn't really a brilliant choice. Being proactive about setting your own goals makes it much less likely that you will succumb to the temptation to let someone else make your career decisions for you!

MAKING IT WORK IN PRACTICE

Goal setting
Go back to the exercise from the last chapter (p. 32) where you wrote down your vision for 'success'. This is the starting point for your long-term goal planning. What would you need to achieve to feel that you were successful? Be specific: what does that look like? What will you be doing, where will you be living, how much will you be earning, who will you be with? What's your timescale for your plan? What do you need to start doing now to help you get there?

Visualising what you need to help you achieve your vision of success will help you identify what you need to do on the road to getting there.

Medium-term goals (one to five years)

If long-term goals are the ones that spell out your personal vision for success, then medium-term goals (by which I mean anything from one to five years), are what will give you the structure to get there. So, if your aim is to get to the top of your industry, you need to know the route to take. What are the progression steps you need to make, and how quickly can you move from step to step? If your financial goal is to retire at 50, you need to work out what size of pension you will need, how much you need to save over the coming years and how you're going to do that. Breaking your long-term goals down into smaller chunks will help you focus more clearly on what you need to achieve each year, or during each stage of your career.

Short-term goals (monthly, weekly, daily)

Finally, your short-term goals are the bread-and-butter of your career progression. It doesn't matter how ambitious you are, or what grand plans you have for the future, if you don't knuckle down and take action, you're not going to get very far. Setting short-term goals and deadlines is the basis of effective time management – a subject that we'll cover in more detail in Part 3 of this book (p. 197). For now, just acknowledge to yourself how easy it is to let a week, a month, even a year go by without doing anything to propel you further forward towards your long-term aims. That's why you need to break your goals down into small chunks, so that you can measure your progress on a regular basis.

REAL LIFE

My friends Brett and Debbie have a great approach to goal-setting. Twice a year, they take themselves off to a nice hotel for the weekend, where they review the last six months and plan for the next six. Brett runs his own business, and Debbie is a professional actress, so they have very busy lives. But regularly taking time out to 'take stock' of where their business and careers are going, and to plan when they are going to take holidays and so on, helps to keep them on track and in control. They come back from their weekends away re-energised and re-focused.

Some more tips on goals

So, we're agreed that goal-setting is the best way of ensuring that you achieve your aims. But how do you actually make it work in practice? Here are a few tips.

- **Write your goals down.** The more concrete your goals, the more likely you are to take action – and therefore to achieve them. The format doesn't matter – it might be a list, or a mind-map, or a spreadsheet. I read recently about a guy who has put together a PowerPoint presentation of his goals – including pictures of the house and car he wants to own – and looks at it first thing every morning. Maybe this would work for you, maybe not! But just make sure you write your goals down somehow. If they're just vague notions in your head, you'll never commit to doing anything to achieve them.

- **Goals aren't an end in themselves.** They're simply a way of recording the actions you need to take, and measuring your progress. Don't spend more time setting and monitoring your goals than you do working to achieve them. When I was at school and university, I'd spend hours writing out detailed timetables for my exam revision. That wasn't actually doing much to achieve my goal – passing my exams – it was more of a displacement activity. Don't let your focus on planning or refining your goals distract you from taking action to fulfil them.

- **Review your goals regularly.** Not just to see what progress you've made towards them – although this is important – but to think about whether your goals themselves are changing. We're human beings, not robots, and our priorities, plans and circumstances change over time. Your goals are a snapshot of your position and your aims at any one point in time – it's therefore a good idea to review them on a regular basis.

Goal-setting is not some rigid, one-dimensional process. It's an effective way of giving structure to your life, your career and your day-to-day activity. But it's important to allow for some flexibility along the way. The irony is that having goals, and knowing what you're aiming for, will allow you to make the most of opportunities that unexpectedly come your way – something we'll look at in the next chapter.

IN A NUTSHELL

- Remember the saying 'failing to plan is planning to fail'. You need to identify your long-term goals so that you're clear about what you're trying to achieve in and through your work.

- Review your goals regularly. Situations and priorities change, so stay flexible.

- Goal setting doesn't achieve anything by itself. You need to back up your planning with action.

If you'd like to learn more about goal setting, I recommend:
Stephen R. Covey, *The 7 Habits of Highly Effective People,* Simon & Schuster Ltd, 2004.

The 'bible' for business and personal planning. The writing style is a little dense and anecdote-heavy, but well worth persevering with.

Look for opportunities

People who excel at work don't leave it to chance. They know where they're headed and they work hard to create opportunities to take them closer to their goals. Sometimes, though, chance has a part to play. And being clear about your goals and objectives will help you not just to make your own opportunities to shine, but to take advantage of any unexpected circumstances that arise.

Why opportunities matter

Opportunities matter because, however fleeting or unplanned, they can have a much bigger single impact on your career and career progression than just doing your job – however excellently – is likely to have. Being good at your job is the foundation-stone for shining at work, but on its own it's unlikely to be enough. The skills and approaches that we will look at in Part 2 of this book (p. 59) will greatly increase your chances of excelling at work – but often it's the one-off opportunities that we come across or create that become our 'career-defining' moments, the stages where we take a big step forward.

Two kinds of opportunity

In the last chapter, we talked about the importance of having a career vision, a plan and goals to get you there. For much of the time – I'm not going to deny this! – meeting your goals and objectives is about hard slog. If you want to write a book, you have to sit down and write it word by word, chapter by chapter. If you want to become an expert in tax law (some people do), you have to put in the hours of study and sit the exams. In fact, achieving your goals usually involves a lot of hard work. But there's one technique that you can use to boost your prospects, accelerate your career and speed up the rate at which you reach your goals: by being alert to opportunities and acting on them.

In my view, there are two kinds of opportunity: those that unexpectedly come your way, and those that you seek out for yourself. Perhaps we could describe them as 'passive' and 'proactive' opportunities. Examples of passive opportunities might be getting a call from a head-hunter, being offered a secondment opportunity, your boss resigning, getting promoted or going on maternity leave. All of these situations potentially have an impact on your career path and progression, even though they weren't initiated by you and are essentially out of your control.

Proactive opportunities, on the other hand, occur when you yourself take the initiative. That might be by suggesting new ways of working or methods to cut costs, for example, or volunteering to manage a new project. These are the occasions when you spot the chance to accelerate your career, raise your profile or enhance your reputation.

Whether an opportunity arises unexpectedly, or it's one that you have worked to create, they all have some features in common. By understanding what these are, you'll put yourself in a much stronger position to capitalise on opportunities that come your way – and to engineer them for yourself.

Create interactions

Opportunities are about interactions. Put simply, that means that they're about people. The bottom line in business is that it's people who create opportunities for other people. To give you a straightforward example, one of the most frequently quoted statistics within the career coaching world is that around 75% of jobs are never advertised. I suspect that this percentage varies according to industry, but it's certainly true that a high proportion of jobs are filled by word of mouth or through someone's personal recommendation. So the number of opportunities to progress and develop that you're likely to come across will be directly related to the quality and quantity of your professional relationships.

Be visible

Opportunities also rely on visibility. It doesn't matter how good you are at your job, how keen you are to progress or to take on extra responsibilities or try something new: if no one knows about you, you're not going to get too many approaches! People need to have you in their sight-line before they can put opportunities your way.

So, you need to make sure that you are visible. That doesn't mean cosying up to the managing director or other senior people, but it does mean concentrating on building your networks and your relationships, with peers and colleagues as well as people higher up the organisation. You should also remember to make contact with people outside your organisation too.

Finally, there's not much point in being visible if you're not also credible. You want people to talk about you – but only in a good way! That means being good at your core job, knowing your organisation and industry sector and being prepared to voice ideas and opinions, and being ultra-professional at all times.

Responding to opportunities

Let's look in a bit more detail at how best to handle opportunities – or potential opportunities – that come your way unexpectedly. As we've seen above, these often arise because of organisational changes – someone moves on, the business sets up a new division, and so on. Be aware that these kinds of opportunity can be quite fleeting – your initial response when you are invited to apply for a new role, or take a secondment to another part of the business, for example, is critical. If you're too cagey in your response, the chance might just slip through your fingers.

Equally, not every opportunity will be right for you. It's easy to fall into the trap of being flattered that you've been asked, but if the role or responsibility that's being offered to you isn't one that fits into your longer-term plans, then you need to be cautious. That said, sometimes one opportunity leads to another, so you never know where saying yes might ultimately take you. So, how do you manage that conflict? My advice is to be as open as possible to opportunities that come your way, and not to turn anything down without at least having a proper conversation about it.

However, don't allow yourself to be rushed into anything: negotiate the time to think the opportunity through carefully, in terms of your longer-term goals as well as any short-term benefits for your career. That way, you're less likely to get pushed into something that you actually don't want to do or aren't able to deliver – which will simply make you look flaky or, worse, incompetent.

So, take the time to assess unexpected opportunities properly. But recognise that this could be a career-defining moment. Be as deft, flexible and visionary in your outlook as you can.

MAKING IT WORK IN PRACTICE

Assessing opportunities

Take 20 minutes or so and sketch out a 'timeline' of your career to date. What prompted you to make each of the moves that you did – was it something that you planned, or did an opportunity arise unexpectedly? Looking back, which were the opportunities that you now wish you hadn't pursued? Were there any that you 'passed' on that in hindsight you wish you had taken? What do your actions tell you about your response to opportunities? Do you tend to be too hasty in taking action, or too cautious? Being aware of how you tend to react to opportunities will help you to make better decisions in the future.

Creating opportunities

You might be reading this and thinking 'That's all very well, but I've never been approached about a new role/promotion/chance to get involved in other areas of the business'. Well, if that's the case, you need to get to work on finding your own opportunities! Below is a list of key actions that will increase your chances of creating opportunities to shine. Each of them is dealt with in detail later in the book, so if you want more information now, then turn to the relevant chapter (indicated in brackets).

- **Build your network** (Chapter 9). Probably the single most important action you can take to bring more opportunity your way. The more people you know, and who know you, the more likely that you'll hear about interesting openings.

- **Raise your profile** (Chapter 10). We've mentioned this already, but it merits a chapter of its own. It's not enough just to know lots of people: you have to be known by, and visible to, the right people. And they need to know what you do, what you're good at and what you're interested in.

- **Keep informed** (Chapter 16). If you are well-briefed about your organisation, your industry sector and the wider world of business, curious about the world around you, and open to new ideas and learning, you'll start to spot all sorts of connections – and opportunities – that might otherwise pass you by.

- **Be influential** (Chapter 21). Your opinion needs to count. You need to be – or become – someone that people turn to for advice, ideas and support.

- **Develop charisma** (Chapter 24). People want to be around charismatic people, people who make them feel good about themselves and make the world seem a better, happier, more interesting place. Charismatic people are the first ones that others think of when opportunities arise.

Being alert, and open, to opportunities should be a key element of your career management strategy. Careers are funny things: they don't always pan out how we expect them to, however much we plan.

REAL LIFE

I've already written about my friend David, the corporate communications professional, but I'm going to bring him up again because David is a great example of someone who takes advantage of opportunities – and creates his own. Because he's extremely talented and a great networker, people talk about him a lot – and that means that he gets frequent approaches from head-hunters. He's worked hard to get himself to the position where opportunities just keep coming his way. Some people might say he's 'lucky', but in my opinion luck has nothing to do with it. He's hardworking, an expert in his field and is exceptionally charismatic – that's why opportunity comes knocking.

Making sure that you are in the market for opportunities will help you broaden your options and increase the likelihood of finding ways in which you can really shine.

IN A NUTSHELL

- Be open to new opportunities – they can often be career-defining moments.

- Opportunities come from other people, so to be in the market you need to be both credible and visible.

- You don't have to take up an opportunity just because it has come your way, but be clear about why you are turning it down.

- Make sure you work at creating your own opportunities as well as looking for those that come your way.

Make the most of where you are now

How you perform in your current role is the best measure of how far – and quickly – your career is likely to progress. Don't wait until you've landed the 'perfect' job before you start implementing all the strategies and tactics in this book. Make the most of where you are now – but be alert to changes in circumstances that tell you it really is time to move on.

Make the most of 'now'

You picked up this book because you want to learn how to shine at work – at least, I assume that's why you picked it up! But it never ceases to amaze me, when I work with clients or talk at seminars and workshops, how many people hold back from giving their best – because they're not yet in their 'perfect' job. Time and again I hear comments like 'Once I get promoted, I'll start building up my network' or, 'When I move jobs, I'll sort out my time management'. Because they're not in their dream job, they're happy to coast along and get by with doing the minimum. But what they haven't realised is that being brilliant at the job you're currently in is the key to getting the job you really want.

Don't allow yourself to fall into the trap of saying 'I'll do "XXX" much better in my new job'. I know it's tempting, especially if you've been in your current role for a while: you probably think it would look a bit 'odd' if you suddenly start changing your behaviour at work. After all, the people you work with are used to how you are and the way you do things, so why rock the boat? And wouldn't it be embarrassing – not to mention risky – to admit that you haven't always been working to the best of your ability?

Well, if you want a fresh start to your career, the time for that start is now. Now is the time to make an honest assessment of your strengths and weaknesses, to decide where you need to make more effort and begin to shine. It doesn't matter if the job you're currently in isn't where you want to be forever. It's where you are now, so make the most of it. Use your current job as your training ground, where you really polish up your act and start to shine. Even if you're ready to move on from your current job, and are actively looking for a new role, don't tread water in the meantime. Put as much effort as you can into being as good as you can right now.

Giving your best now

I've said it before, but it's worth repeating: your career is a journey. Enjoy the trip, rather than just looking forward to the final destination.

You should make it your mission to do your professional best at every job that you do – even ones that you might just regard as a 'stepping stone' to where you really want to get to. However dull the work you might be doing, you can always find ways to shine. Take every opportunity you can to implement the approaches and tactics in the following chapters: these are the attitudes and behaviours that are going to accelerate your career progress and get you to where you want to be that much more quickly. They're also the attitudes and behaviours that will help you get as much satisfaction and enjoyment as you can out of where you currently are. In fact, I could be controversial and suggest that you shouldn't even be thinking about moving on or up, until you've mastered the skills and habits set out in Part 2!

The main point of this chapter is that you don't have to wait until 'tomorrow' to start boosting your performance at work. As we know, tomorrow never comes! Get started now on making the most of every day at work and giving it your very best.

MAKING IT WORK IN PRACTICE

Making the most of now

As you read through Part 2 of this book, make a note of the two or three most important actions you can start to take now to improve your performance at work. Maybe you need to get out there and do some networking, or focus on learning a new skill, or improve your time management. Whatever your priorities, start putting changes in place as soon as you can. Shining in your current role is the best way to prepare yourself for the role you really want.

Knowing when it's time to move on

Despite what I've stressed above – that your current role, however temporary you feel it is, offers you plenty of scope to hone your professional skills – there usually comes a point when you know it's definitely time to move on. The triggers for this moment can broadly be described as 'external' and 'internal'. External triggers might be a company restructuring that limits your chances of progression, or your boss being replaced by the person with a reputation for being a bully and a nightmare to work for. Internal triggers are more about your own attitude to work: perhaps you've simply become a bit bored, can't see any prospects, or just aren't finding it fun anymore. Let's look at some of these triggers, and how to respond to them, in a little more detail.

'I hate my new boss'

Not getting on with the boss is one of the most common reasons for people deciding to change jobs. That's entirely understandable: your manager is likely to be the person who has the most impact on your work and your enjoyment of it. But before you throw in the towel, just make sure that the problem isn't you! Most of us are resistant to change, and a new manager coming on the scene can cause all sorts of upheaval: they'll probably have a different way of doing things, different priorities and a different management style. Be honest with yourself: if your relationship with your previous boss was very good, have you allowed yourself to become just a little complacent? Ask yourself what you can learn from your new boss. Take the time and effort to find out how they like to work, and to respond accordingly. For example, perhaps their approach is quite formal and they like to be given written briefings in advance of meetings, whereas your previous boss was happy with informal verbal updates. Do your best to build a good relationship. But be aware that a good relationship with your manager is critical for your own profile and progression so, if you really can't make it work, then you might be better off working for someone else!

'I can't get a promotion or a pay rise'

This is a problem that many of my clients encountered as a result of the recession. Cutbacks and internal restructuring have meant pay freezes and a reduction in prospects for promotion or other development. It can be really frustrating when you feel that your career is grinding to a halt, and there's not much you can do about it. But there *are* things you can do: talk to your manager about taking on a special project, extending your area of responsibility (even without a pay rise!) or maybe making a sideways move to get experience of a different area of the business. Think about ways in which you could add value to the company as well as to your CV – perhaps you could help to mentor junior staff, for example. Do explore all your options for further development before you finally decide to up sticks and move on. Give your employers the opportunity to show that they value you, even if they can't reward you in cash or promotion.

'I just don't care about it any more'

It's not uncommon to lose interest in something that once excited you. In fact, that's why many people have several careers throughout their working life: they simply get a bit bored with the same old routine and subject matter. Again, the simple rule of exploring all your options applies: think about ways in which you could freshen up your role or learn about different areas of the business. But, if you find yourself increasingly getting the 'Sunday night blues', and can't summon up much enthusiasm for what you're doing, then it may well be time to look for pastures new.

The secret to making a rational decision about whether it's time to move on is to assess how much scope you have to influence or change the situation. If it's not fixable, then chances are it's time for you to look elsewhere. But do make sure that you explore all your options before you make a final decision. And be especially honest about your own role in the 'problem': if you're feeling stressed and overwhelmed because you're not well-organised at work, for example, moving to another job probably isn't going to change that. Draw a distinction between situations that you can – and should – move away from, and problems that are about your own attitude and behaviour – which you'll probably end up taking with you if you do move on. In short, be clear about what you can – and should – try to fix, and do it before you go anywhere else.

IN A NUTSHELL

- Don't wait until you've landed your dream job before adopting the attitudes and behaviours that will make you shine. Start raising your game now.

- Doing a brilliant job where you are is the best way to prepare for the job you really want.

- Know when it's time to move on, but make sure you consider all the options at your current position before you make your final decision.

If you'd like to learn more about making the most of where you are now, I recommend:

Marshall Goldsmith, *What Got You Here Won't Get You There*, Profile Books Ltd, 2008.

A superb analysis of the attitudes and behaviours that hold us back in the workplace. Very highly recommended.

MANAGING YOUR CAREER

In Part 1, we looked at how the level of success that you achieve at work is determined, to a large extent, by how good the 'fit' is between you, your values and strengths, and the nature of the work you do. But there's more to it than that. People who really shine at work are the ones who consistently display the behaviours that guarantee a stellar reputation. In short, this comes down to how well they know their industry and organisation, and how deftly they manage relationships. So, in this part of the book, let's look in more detail at the behaviours and approaches that are critical to your success at work.

Build your network

Relationships are the bedrock of your career, where you'll
find it really is 'who you know, not what you know'. In a
world where technology is making the business dealings
we have with others more remote, the people who stand
out are the ones who take the time to get personal. You
need to network widely, with groups as well as individuals.
But stay focused on what your networking objectives
are. Above all, remember that networking is a two-way
process: it's about giving as well as getting.

Why networking matters

Social networking, online networking, business networking – 'networking' is one of the 21st century's buzzwords. And there are very good reasons for that. Of course we live in a time where technology has made it easier and easier to get, and stay, in touch with more and more people. Ironically though, technology has also served to de-personalise many of our relationships, whether professional or personal: as a colleague who would probably describe himself as 'old school' once moaned to me years ago: 'Email is killing the art of conversation'.

And, funnily enough, that's precisely why networking is more important now than it has ever been. In a world where we are bombarded on a daily basis with emails, advertising and information overload, the people who stand out are those who still find the time to make personal, face-to-face contact with others. And the reason that's so important is simply this: relationships are the basis of any business. The quality of your relationships will determine the quality of your career. If you do only one thing to help build and develop your career, make it this: build your network.

REAL LIFE

My friend Jonathan is one of the best networkers that I know. He spends enormous amounts of time going to events, meeting people, following up with them afterwards, and – which is especially valuable – putting his contacts in touch with each other. As a result, his contact book reads like 'Who's Who' – politicians, entrepreneurs, famous business people, you name it. He's really made networking into an art, and it's paid off for him. Through his network, he was offered his dream job in consultancy. And he uses his network to bring in new business, keep himself up-to-date with developments and ensure that he stays at the top of his game.

Networking to build your career

Most people think of networking in the context of looking for a job, or for new clients and customers. But successful networking can do much more for your career than simply helping you to find a job in the first place. Through networking, you will build relationships, increase your knowledge, make connections and bring fresh ideas to your work. The more people you know, the more wisdom and information you have access to, and the less you will have to re-invent the wheel.

Overcoming your nerves

People often shy away from networking because they perceive it as 'pushy', 'artificial' or just embarrassing. But none of these feelings need apply, if you get your approach right. For me, the secret is to look at networking as a long-term game, and a reciprocal one. In other words, you are aiming to extend your contacts, and meet a whole range of interesting new people who may be able to help you at some point in the future – and whom you may be able to help in turn. Networking is about increasing your 'reach' or 'personal web', and it's about learning – about people, about your own and other industry sectors, sometimes even about yourself.

Growing your network

Networking works because business is about relationships. It also works because people enjoy talking about themselves and their experiences, and they like to be asked for advice! Here are some tips for growing a valuable network.

Know your networking objectives

Whether your objective is to find a new job, identify business development opportunities, or learn more about issues affecting your role or sector, be clear what you are looking to achieve from your networking activity. Otherwise, it's all too easy to spend lots of time socialising without any real benefit for your career. Your networking objectives should inform the kind of networking that you do: for example, if you want to build your knowledge of your industry, then industry events and seminars are what you should be focusing on. If you're looking for a new position in a different industry, then you need to make sure you're meeting lots of people outside your current industry sector.

Network widely

If you haven't had a structured approach to networking up till now, by all means start with your friends, family and work colleagues. In practical terms, to make a start building your network you should go through your diary, contacts book and email history – and even Facebook and other networking sites you might have signed up to, such as LinkedIn. Who do you know that you haven't spoken to for a while? Get in touch and arrange to meet for coffee or lunch. Look at the process as relationship-building, and making or renewing friendships, and it will seem a lot less daunting. As you re-connect with people you already know, they in turn will point you in the direction of other people with whom it would be useful for you to get in touch.

But you shouldn't limit your networking activity to people you already know, or people only within your own industry sector. You're more likely to gain fresh ideas and perspectives from people whose jobs are quite different from your own, so try to move outside your comfort zone and make contact with people you may not know as well or who work in an entirely different sector from you. And think about using a range of networking techniques: online forums, one-to-one meetings, and attending bigger events should all be part of the mix.

Make contact with groups, not just individuals

One way of helping to grow your network is to tap into existing groups or business forums – groups relevant to your industry, or business forums local to your area – so that you have the opportunity to make several new contacts in one go. But you need to manage this well: it can be time-consuming, so choose your business networks with care. And don't fall into the trap of thinking that the more business cards you give out – or collect – the more productively you have spent your time.

Concentrate on having a few genuine discussions rather than rushing around the room trying to say hello to everyone. If the conversations that you do have are useful, that's an indication that the group as a whole is worth staying in touch with.

Think about what you can give back in return

Networking is a two-way process so, when you meet someone new, think about what, or who, you know that might be helpful to your new contact. Spend time and effort maintaining the relationships that you make. It might not be possible for you to keep in regular contact with absolutely everyone that you meet but do, as a minimum, stay in close touch with your 'golden contacts' – those people who put the most business your way, or offer the soundest advice, or have strong networks of their own, for example.

Keep good records

You might think that you'll remember everyone you meet and what they tell you, but, trust me, you won't! Keep records of whom you meet and when, what they do and any key points from your conversation. Get yourself a set of index cards, or – if you're really serious about building and maintaining your network – invest in some customer relationship management software. Develop the discipline of writing short notes about everyone you meet – and, of course, their contact details!

MAKING IT WORK IN PRACTICE

Networking

So you've signed up for a networking event – and maybe you're feeling a bit nervous. How do you make sure that you get the most out of the evening? Try these tips.

- **Get there in good time.** *You'll feel less daunted if there are fewer people there when you arrive, rather than walking into a crowded room when the event is already in full swing.*

- **Take the initiative.** *Help with pouring drinks or offering food around – it's a good ice-breaker and gives you something to do* *with your hands! Try to put yourself in the mindset of a 'host' – focus on other people, not yourself.*

- **Look for people on their own, or groups of three or four.** *The hardest conversation to break into is often one between two people so look for larger groups or for people on their own. Wait for a pause in the conversation, and then introduce yourself and make a comment relevant to what's being talked about.*

- **Don't cop out by spending the whole evening with one group.** *Move around and make sure that you talk to a range of people.*

- **Get comfortable with ending conversations as well as starting them.** *Just say something simple and straightforward like 'It's been lovely to meet you, there's a couple of other people I'd like to catch up with', and move on – making sure you have their contact details, of course.*

- **Don't try to do business at the event.** *If you meet someone interesting with whom you'd like to follow up, get their business card and ask if you can drop them an email or give them a call in the next few days. And make sure that you do!*

It's well worth taking time and effort firstly to think about your networking strategy, and then to put it into practice. Relationships are the bedrock of any business – and any career. Remember, in the end it's all about people.

IN A NUTSHELL

- Networking is probably the single most important thing you can do to boost your profile and your career.

- Think about networking as a two-way process: it's as much about what you can give as what you can get.

- Be clear about your networking objectives, and keep good records.

If you'd like to learn more about the art of networking, I recommend: Carole Stone, *Networking: The art of making friends,* Vermilion Press, 2001.

A light-hearted but practical guide by the 'queen' of networking. The emphasis is more on social than business networking, but plenty of great advice applicable to all networking situations.

www.ecademy.com. The original online business networking community, founded in 1998 and still going strong. Online networking is complemented by physical networking events and presentations.

www.linkedin.com. Free online network for business professionals. Has less of a US focus than ecademy, and I personally find it easier to use.

10

Raise your profile

It doesn't matter how good you are at your job if people aren't aware of that fact – or of you! Raise your head above the parapet and make sure you are visible at work. Increase the amount of face-to-face time you spend with colleagues and others in the organisation. Get involved, be a 'can-do' person and never let your professional standards slip.

It's not just about networking...

In Chapter 7, we discussed the importance of your visibility in helping you to access and create professional opportunities. Let's look in more detail at the best ways of improving your visibility – in other words, how to raise your profile.

We've already looked at the importance of networking in Chapter 9 and as we saw there's no doubt that networking is an invaluable way of increasing your visibility, as well as improving your knowledge and your access to opportunities. But it's not the only approach to raising your profile: there are lots of other things you can do to help get yourself noticed – in a good way. Many of these activities and approaches merit a chapter to themselves, and are therefore covered in more detail later. Here, for those of you looking for a quick guide, are the best things you can do at work – and outside of it – to help make yourself more visible.

Be seen

It may sound obvious but you'd be surprised how many times I've heard a client complain that they don't feel 'noticed' at work – when they're not doing anything to get themselves noticed! Just doing a good job simply isn't enough: a good job is what you're paid to do. If you spend your day sitting at your computer, not interacting with anyone beyond your immediate colleagues, it really doesn't matter how high the quality of your work is – you're unlikely to register on the radar of the people who matter in terms of your profile and progress within the company.

So, you need to get out there and make yourself visible. Here are some ideas about how to do this.

- **Think 'face-to-face'**. It's all too easy to 'hide' behind your email rather than lifting the telephone to talk to someone or, better still, going to see them. Have you ever sent an email to someone who was sitting just a few feet away from you? We've probably all done it – and in some cases email is the best medium. But nothing can beat the art of conversation. So make an effort to ensure that at least 5%–10% of your interactions are face-to-face and personal.

- **Speak up in meetings**. Many of us hate public speaking of any kind, and will leave it to others to contribute in meetings. Of course, you don't want to build a reputation as a motor-mouth who speaks up whether they have anything useful to contribute or not, but try to find one useful point to make in any meeting you attend – otherwise what's the point in your being there?

- **Volunteer**. If your boss has a new pet project where he needs some help with the admin, volunteer, even if it's not in your job description. If one of the new trainees is seeking a mentor, volunteer. Become known as someone who's prepared to help out for no extra reward. And don't just volunteer for the 'glamorous' opportunities, either. Be prepared to get stuck in even if the task is dull. Of course, make sure that you don't over-commit yourself or your real work will suffer. But becoming known as a 'can-do' person who's prepared to go the extra mile can work wonders for your reputation and profile.

- **Participate**. Whether it's the annual company fundraiser for charity, or the departmental away day – play a part. Get involved in events that other people are planning – offer to help, even if it's in a behind-the-scenes capacity. Colleagues doing the organising will be genuinely grateful, and you'll get to meet new people or get to know your boss and team-mates better.

- **Socialise**. In a similar vein, don't be the person who slopes off straight after work every day of the week. No one is suggesting that your colleagues need to become part of your extended family, but socialising with them occasionally will help you to get to know them better, as well as opening up opportunities for you to meet people in other areas of the business. Most companies or organisations have one or two 'favourite' watering holes, so you never know who you might bump into. Needless to say, however informal and social the environment, you still need to be on good behaviour! No one wants to discover, too late, that the person they spent half-an-hour rambling drunkenly to the night before is actually the new Vice-Chairman. (And yes, I am speaking from personal experience on that one!).

REAL LIFE

My friend Neil is one of the most 'visible' people that I know. If there's an event going on at work, chances are he's been involved in organising it. If there's a party or social event, he'll be there. If he can get away from his desk and talk to people face-to-face, he'll do it. As a result, he's known by everyone in his organisation, from the very top to the very bottom. And he's been promoted twice in the last three years.

Become a 'go-to' person

In Chapter 4 we covered the value of carving out a 'niche' for yourself: an area, or areas, of expertise which mean that other people come to you for knowledge and advice. Becoming known as a 'go-to' person is a great way of raising your profile, not least because people whom you've helped will most likely tell other people. But you don't have to spend hours of your free time becoming an expert on all areas of your business. There are a number of straightforward ways in which you can make yourself more visible.

- **Pass on useful information**. So, if you spot an interesting article in the press or a trade magazine about your industry sector, think who else might find it of interest and send them a copy, with a short covering note or email. They're likely to be impressed at your efficiency and flattered that you thought of them. One tip: don't circulate articles from press or other publications that everyone in the organisation reads anyway. You'll just look a little desperate! Instead, keep an eye on publications – and blogs – that are relevant, but not necessarily core, to your industry: *Management Today*, for example, or *Marketing Week* if you're in the PR industry, as opposed to *PR Week*, which everyone reads anyway.

- **Be an 'introducer'.** If you've started to build up your professional network, this is another way not only of raising your profile, but of being genuinely useful to others at work. Who have you met that one of your colleagues might find it really useful to get in touch with? Who's in your network that other people might find a helpful resource, either professionally or personally? That person might be a financial adviser, a lawyer, a personal trainer, a plumber, you name it. When people need the help of a professional, they much prefer a word-of-mouth recommendation. So become the person who knows who to go to.

Be professional

Again, this sounds pretty obvious, but the secret is to be *consistently* professional: you never know who's watching, or who you're going to bump into unexpectedly. You can't afford to have an 'off' day! Particular areas to concentrate on include the following.

- **Your appearance.** We'll discuss this more in a later chapter (see p. 190), but the rule of thumb is to dress every day as if you had an important meeting. Your diary might be empty just now, but that doesn't mean that something won't crop up at the last minute – you need to stand in for your boss at a presentation or reception, for example, or a client brings forward an appointment. Looking the part at all times is a good way to get yourself noticed for positive reasons. That doesn't mean you have to spend a fortune on your work outfits – in fact, no one likes a 'flashy' dresser - but you do need to be neat and well-groomed.

- **Your attitude**. Again, you need to exude professionalism at all times. I do hope it goes without saying, but this means: never losing your temper, retaining your sense of humour even when things are going pear-shaped, and always treating clients and colleagues with respect. Remembering the common courtesies: 'please', 'thank you' and a cheerful 'good morning' to whomever you meet in the lift will make sure you always give out the right impression. Foster these habits so that they become second nature, not just a routine that you roll out in front of senior staff.

- **Don't hide your light under a bushel**. If you've done a great job, and a client or colleague writes or emails to say thank you, show it to your boss. You do need to avoid coming across as a 'show-off', of course; the best way to do this is to say something like 'Isn't it great that so-and-so is happy with our service?'. That way, you're reflecting the praise onto the organisation, not just yourself. But it's important for your profile that people know when you have done something really well.

HOW TO MAKE IT WORK IN PRACTICE

Raising your profile

You might be thinking 'If I try to do everything suggested in this chapter, I'll never have time to do my real job!' You don't have to do all of the things I've suggested – and certainly not all at once (except for being professional, of course: that's a full-time activity). But do try to incorporate some of these activities into your week. Bear in mind, though, that you need to be consistent: better to do a few things on a regular basis than to embark on a flurry of activity that you can't maintain, so that you quickly fall under the radar again. You don't want people saying 'Whatever happened to (your name)…?'!

IN A NUTSHELL

- You can't shine if you're not visible! People need to see what you have to offer.

- Don't just stick within your own 'silo' at work – look for opportunities to get involved in other areas, both professionally and socially.

- Be consistently professional in your standards and appearance. Other people need to like what they see and know that it's not just a one-off.

If you'd like to learn more about raising your profile, I recommend: Amanda Vickers, Steve Bavister and Jackie Smith, *Personal Impact: What it takes to make a difference*, Pearson Education Ltd, 2009.

A very practical guide to raising your profile and increasing your personal impact. Lots of exercises and case studies to illustrate the points being made.

11

Find – and be – a mentor

A mentor can be a great boost to your career. Benefiting from the experience of someone who's been there before you is one of the best ways to learn, and tapping into someone else's network is the quickest way to build your own. And, in turn, acting as a mentor for someone else will help to develop your management skills and raise your profile.

What can a mentor do for me?

I advise all the clients that I work with to find themselves a mentor. Why? Because having a good mentor is a great way of helping yourself to excel at your own work – and to get noticed for it. A mentor is simply someone with more experience or knowledge than you, who can be an adviser, a sounding-board and a morale booster.

Your mentor can help you avoid mistakes, assist you in developing ideas or new approaches and help you raise your profile inside your organisation and beyond.

A mentor can help you professionally in a whole range of ways, such as:

- **improving your knowledge of your company, organisation or sector.** A mentor who is more senior than you, either within your own organisation, or in a related business sector, can be a brilliant source of knowledge and learning. For example, they can help you gain a wider understanding of how your business operates and what the key challenges and priorities for the sector are. In short, a mentor with wider and more senior experience can help you to gain a 'bird's-eye view' of the industry you're working in

- **tackling specific problems.** When you come across a hurdle at work – perhaps you're struggling with a particular report or presentation, or you're feeling overwhelmed by your workload – a mentor can be a great sounding-board to help you get 'unstuck'

- **boosting your morale.** Sometimes you just need someone to perk you up a bit, help you get back on track and regain your positivity. A mentor who has been 'around the block' a few times will have the experience to help you put problems and setbacks into perspective, and to encourage you to focus on your strengths and achievements

- **being your champion**. Particularly if your mentor works in the same organisation as you, they can be someone who helps you to raise your profile and get yourself noticed. A senior colleague who takes you under their wing, and talks to other people about you (in a good way of course!) is an invaluable asset to your career.

What's in it for them?

A mentoring relationship can be just as satisfying for your mentor as for you. People become mentors for all sorts of reasons: perhaps they want to 'give something back'; maybe they are keen to share their knowledge and experience, and bring an extra dimension to their own job; or they may simply enjoy being turned to for advice and held in high regard! In any case, successful people will understand the importance of getting support, and will probably themselves have used and benefited from a mentor at some point in their career.

Finding a mentor

So, how do you go about finding yourself a mentor? First of all, think about what you would most like to gain from the relationship. If you're keen to expand your knowledge of the company or your business sector, for example, then seek out a mentor higher up in your own organisation. If you're looking for someone who will help to keep you focused, positive and on-track, then you could look outside your own organisation – your mentor's attitude will be more important than their industry knowledge. In fact, choosing a mentor who operates in a different sector to yours can be valuable as often they will have fresh ideas and insights that you can apply to your own role. And you don't have to limit yourself to just one mentor – you may be able to find two or three different people who will be prepared to spend some time with you now and again, and who can offer you different kinds of advice and support.

You may already have someone whom you turn to for advice from time to time, and who is effectively fulfilling the role of mentor, it's just that you haven't formalised the relationship as a 'mentoring' one. If you don't have someone like this, think about the people whom you really look up to and respect, both within your organisation and outside it. Who are your role models? Who would you like to be like? Who can you really learn from? Approach them and ask them if they would be prepared to be your mentor. It's that straightforward – after all, the worst they can say is no! Chances are they'll say yes but, even if they do refuse – perhaps because they are just too busy – they'll be flattered to have been asked, and they will remember you should you come across them again at a later date.

Your mentor also needs to be someone you not only trust and respect, but whom you feel comfortable with. There's no point approaching someone so senior that you will get tongue-tied every time you meet with them! You need to be able to talk with them honestly and openly about your challenges and problems, otherwise they're not going to be able to help you much. So make sure your chosen mentor is someone with whom you have – or can build – a strong rapport.

MAKING IT WORK IN PRACTICE

Finding a mentor
When choosing a mentor, look for someone who's got around 10 years' more experience than you do. They'll have a wealth of knowledge for you to draw on, but will still be able to remember how they felt at the stage of their career that you're now at. They're also likely to have plenty of friends and colleagues who are more senior than you, to whom they may be able to introduce you, helping you to grow your network upwards.

Managing the mentor relationship

The secret of managing a mentor relationship well is to get the balance right between turning to them for support when you need it, and not putting pressure on the relationship by being too 'needy'. A good rule of thumb is to seek to meet up with your mentor roughly every four to six weeks. It's also a good idea to formalise the relationship at the outset: agree with your mentor the kind of support that you're looking for, how often you will meet up and so on.

Make sure, too, that you keep your side of the 'bargain'. Your mentor is giving up their valuable time to focus on you, so make sure that you don't waste it. That means keeping your appointments, turning up on time and not over-running, and being clear and focused about what you want to discuss with them. A meeting with your mentor shouldn't just be a general chat over lunch or a coffee: the discussion should have a purpose.

In terms of the courtesies and practicalities of the relationship, it's a nice gesture for you to make sure you pick up the tab for your coffee, lunch or whatever. It's a small price to pay for the valuable advice you will get in return. And, if your meetings tend to take place in the office or at your mentor's place of work because that's more convenient for them, you should still make sure that you invite them out for a nice lunch every now and again. It's a simple way of demonstrating that you value the relationship and appreciate their time.

REAL LIFE

For a number of years now I have had a brilliant mentor in the form of Jennifer Bryant-Pearson, Managing Director of JBP Ltd, a leading PR company based in Bristol and London. I first met Jennifer when we were both doing some work in the House of Commons, and we hit it off right away. She ticks all the boxes in terms of what I wanted from a mentor. As someone with significantly more business experience than me, I learn so much from her, and see her as a real role model. Although we work in different industry sectors, she always has great ideas for my business, and she gives me a real morale boost every time we meet up. She's also great fun! We meet up every few months or so, and spend the time discussing the development of my business: Jennifer always has ideas for new contacts that I could make, and ways in which I can 'add value' for my customers. I find it a really useful way of taking a step back and looking strategically at how I am spending my time, and where I could more effectively focus my efforts.

Don't just have a mentor: be one too

Getting yourself a mentor can make a huge difference to your career progression. So why not think about giving something back, and in turn mentoring someone more junior than you? As well as giving you a sense of personal satisfaction, mentoring someone can help to improve your management, listening and communication skills, give you a different perspective on your organisation and help to raise your profile. It also looks good on your CV so, no, your motives don't have to be entirely altruistic!

Check with your line manager or HR department as to whether your organisation currently runs a mentoring scheme, perhaps for junior staff, new employees or graduate trainees, for example. Ask how you can get involved. If there are no mentoring schemes already in place, why not think about helping to set one up?

The rules for how you work with the person you mentor are pretty much the same as those discussed above for managing your relationship with your own mentor, just applied in reverse. So: be clear about what you can offer as a mentor, do your best to keep to any appointments made, and remember that your conversations are completely confidential. Work to build up trust and rapport, and you'll be surprised just how satisfying being a mentor can be.

IN A NUTSHELL

- Seek out someone who can be your sounding-board, advisor and champion. Let them help you to shine.

- Choose a mentor whom you respect, trust and can be completely open with.

- Make it a two-way process: mentoring someone more junior than you is a great way of staying in touch with the grass-roots of your organisation.

If you'd like to learn more about mentoring, I recommend:
David Clutterbuck, *Everyone Needs a Mentor: Fostering talent in your organisation,* Chartered Institute of Personnel and Development, 2004.

The classic textbook on mentoring from one of the industry's experts. Geared more towards how to set up a mentoring scheme in your organisation, but has lots of useful information on how to make a mentoring relationship work.

12

Become a leader

Anyone – no matter what their level in an organisation – can be a leader. That's because leadership is as much about attitude as it is about responsibility. Start to cultivate the attributes of leaders: vision and optimism are key. Be a role model for others and you'll truly shine.

What exactly is a leader?

Leadership is one of those qualities that can be difficult to define, but it can be broken into a few key points. The first point to make is that leadership is not the same as management. I've known great leaders who weren't good managers, and terrific managers who weren't really leaders. What's the difference? For me, management is about directing an individual's – or a team's – performance. Leadership, on the other hand, isn't about focusing on the output of individuals, or even a team: rather, it's about vision and the ability to see the big picture. It's also, in my view, about trust and respect. If you wanted to sum up the difference between management and leadership in a nutshell, I would say that management is largely inward-facing (seeking to get the best out of other people) while leadership is outward-facing (looking to the future, and taking other people along with you and your vision).

Leadership is also very much about attitude and behaviour: a leader is someone whom we look up to, whose judgement we respect, someone whom we see as a 'flag-flier' for the organisation.

There's a lot of debate about whether leaders are 'born' or 'made'. My own opinion is that it's probably a mixture of both! We all know people whom we would describe as 'natural' leaders: they're the people that others naturally turn to for advice and direction. But I firmly believe that we can all learn to develop and display leadership qualities. Leadership is as much about mindset as it is about your formal position within the company.

How to be a leader

So much for the theory, but what does that mean for you in practice? Well, if you want to excel at work, you need to be up there at the front – leading. It doesn't matter how junior you are, you can become a leader by being someone whose opinion is sought out and respected, who is seen as a person with vision and a 'can-do' attitude, and who is a real role model for others in the organisation.

Start by leading yourself

No one would follow someone who didn't look as if they knew where they were going, right? So the starting point for becoming a leader is: lead yourself. What does that mean? In my opinion, to lead yourself you need to do some or all of the following.

- **Know where you're going.** You need to have an understanding – a sense of vision, even – of what the future holds for your company or organisation and what that means for your own career. How do you see yourself progressing? Where do you want to be in five or 10 years' time? Know what you – and your organisation – are working towards. That doesn't mean that you should necessarily share your personal career goals with other people, but having a clear sense of direction will mean that you come across as someone with a purposeful approach, someone with drive.

- **Understand your strengths and weaknesses.** None of us is perfect, and very few of us are even good 'all-rounders'. Playing to your strengths – whether that's writing, presenting, or coming up with new ideas – is the best way to establish yourself as the leader in that area. Equally, being prepared to turn to other people who have expertise and experience that you don't is the sign of someone who is confident and comfortable in their own skin: one of the marks of a leader.

- **Invest in your own development.** Leaders keep learning, stretching themselves and developing their skills. Make time to find out more about your industry sector, focus on honing your interpersonal skills, get informed about wider issues in the economy or the political world that are likely to impact on your organisation and its business. All of these are ways in which you can help yourself to become a 'go-to' person: the kind of person that others seek out for advice or information.

Be a 'thought leader'

'Thought leadership' is one of the trendy buzzwords going around these days. What does it mean? In simple terms, it's about spotting trends, opportunities and threats within your industry sector. How is the industry changing? What will be the effects of new technology, new legislation, new patterns of consumer behaviour? And what impact are those likely to have on the way in which your organisation does its business? Reading widely around your subject area – and beyond – will help to keep you informed and up-to-date, as well as giving you ideas for ways in which things can be done better. Don't be shy about sharing your knowledge and input: if you've got a good idea, talk to your line manager, offer to write an article for the in-house newsletter, or take the opportunity at a social function to share your thoughts with someone more senior. Build yourself a reputation for being someone who is up-to-speed, in the know and enthusiastic about the opportunities for your business.

Be a cheerleader

As I've said above, leadership is largely about attitude. What are the behaviours that mark someone out as a leader, regardless of their level of seniority? I'd suggest the following.

- **Be optimistic**. Look for the best in people and situations. Don't over-exaggerate problems or difficulties. Don't say 'This is a disaster!' when it's a minor hiccup that can be solved with a bit of effort. Be upbeat and positive: people will turn to you for direction and moral support – turning you into a leader.

- **View change as an opportunity**. It's fair to say that most of us are naturally risk-averse. We don't like change: it's easier to stick with what's familiar. Yet there's nothing worse than the person whose response to every suggestion is 'no', 'but' or 'however'! Leaders, on the other hand, seize on change as an opportunity to do things better. So whether you're facing a departmental restructuring, a new Chief Executive or some other fundamental change within

your workplace, don't be the naysayer. Be the person who
responds with enthusiasm, and take other people with you.

- **Be collaborative**. Leadership isn't about being in charge.
  It's about playing your part in helping the organisation get
  to where it needs to go. That means working in partnership
  with other people, not competing with them. You won't
  become regarded as a leader by constantly striving to 'win':
  you'll just put people's backs up and gain a reputation for
  being selfish and ruthlessly ambitious.

- **Be a role model**. Make sure that your behaviour at all
  times is something that other people will want to emulate.
  Be positive. Support your boss and colleagues. Keep your
  personal and professional standards high. Be focused,
  energetic, calm under pressure, a nice person to be around.
  Seems like a tall order? Well, it is. But leaders lead by
  setting an example that others want to follow.

REAL LIFE

My friend James is one of life's 'leaders'. He's definitely not
a manager, but he's the first to spot new opportunities for
his company, he's full of optimism and enthusiasm, and he's
brilliant at getting other people on board and taking them
with him. He's passionate about what he does, and his great
talent is to get other people to share his passion and his
vision. That's leadership, in my opinion.

And finally: what leaders *shouldn't* do

I think there's a lot of mythology around what makes a leader: most of
us probably conjure up an image of someone who is driven, ruthless,
maybe even slightly Machiavellian. I hope I've shown above that

the qualities of a leader are rather different from this stereotype. So let's finish this chapter with a few pointers on the things you really shouldn't do if you want to be seen as a leader – regardless of how the Hollywood blockbuster might portray them!

- **You don't need to 'win' all the time.** Leaders are often depicted as 'winners' – people who drive their ideas forward and succeed in influencing others to their way of thinking. And, yes, that is part of being a leader. You can't lead if you don't have ideas and you don't see them through. But you don't have to win every time. A true leader knows which fights are worth winning and which don't really matter.

- **You don't have to add value all the time.** Yes, you need to have areas and issues where you can make a strong contribution, but you don't need to pipe up with your opinion at every single opportunity. Develop a reputation for being knowledgeable in a few areas – not for being a know-it-all.

- **You don't become a leader by putting other people down.** Leadership is, by definition, about being at the front – at least some of the time. But that's not about stepping on, or over, other people on your way to the top. Leaders bring out the best in other people – and know when to surround themselves with, and lean on, people who have skills and knowledge that they don't.

IN A NUTSHELL

- Leadership is as much about your attitude and approach as about your level of seniority in the organisation.

- Leaders have a vision: they know where they and their organisation are heading, and they take other people with them.

- Leaders aren't loners: they collaborate with other people to achieve the organisation's goals.

If you'd like to learn more about being a leader, I recommend:
Steve Radcliffe, *Leadership: Plain and simple*, Financial Times/Prentice Hall, 2009.

A brilliant and straightforward guide to the skills of leadership. Practical, direct and accessible.

13

Support your boss

Your relationship with your boss is critical to your own success at work. Developing a good relationship with your manager will help you to raise your own profile – and do your job better. Learn to look at things from your boss's perspective: what are their priorities? How can you best support them? Be an advocate for them and they will most likely return the favour.

Why your boss matters

Your boss, or line manager, or reporting officer, or however you describe him or her, is the most important person in your professional circle. Why? Because they are your gateway to progression.

Most likely, it is your boss who will conduct your performance appraisal, recommend you for a pay rise or promotion, and – most importantly – talk about you to people higher up the organisation, or outside it. It follows then that your boss is the person whom you most need to impress!

How do you do that? Start by trying to see things from your manager's perspective. They have a wider range of responsibilities than you, and probably more people than just you to manage. Their role is most likely broader, more complex and more visible than yours. While you might spend quite a lot of your working day thinking about your boss, they probably spend less time thinking about you because of everything else they have on their plate.

Valuable employee qualities

Looking at it from your boss's viewpoint, what would be the qualities they most value in an employee? I suggest the following:

- someone who understands their priorities and working style
- someone who makes their job easier, not harder
- someone who makes them look good
- someone who is committed, loyal and trustworthy.

These valuable qualities are the key to handling your boss! Let's look at them in more detail.

Understand their priorities and working style

You can work as hard as you like, but if you're not focusing on the things that are really important to your boss, you're pretty much wasting your time. So you need to know what your boss's key priorities and objectives are. And there's only one way to find out – ask. If you don't do this already, schedule a regular meeting with your boss to discuss your – and their – workload. What should you be concentrating on? What are the tasks that it's really important for you to complete, and what are the areas that might be really interesting to you, but aren't as high on your boss's radar? Like it or not, your boss is going to assess your performance on the basis of what they personally regard as the key tasks – which may not be quite the same as what's on your official job description.

Equally, get to know how your boss likes to work, and match that behaviour. For example, if they are someone who prefers written to oral briefing, make sure that you have notes or a briefing paper for any meeting you have with them – and preferably let them see it in advance. If they are someone who likes to manage with a 'light touch', don't go running to them with every small problem that you encounter – they'll just think you're needy and insecure. On the other hand, if your boss has a tendency to micro-manage (and, yes, I do know how annoying that can be), make sure that you report back to them regularly on your work. The only way you can get a micro-managing boss off your back is to prove to them that you are completely competent and reliable, and constantly to re-assure them. Micro-management is often a sign of insecurity on your boss's part, so you need to do all that you can to make them feel fully confident in you.

Make their job easier, not harder

As I've said above, your boss's job is harder than yours – that's why they get paid more! Do everything that you can to make your boss's life easier. Try to anticipate their needs. If you have access to your boss's diary, make a point of checking it at the beginning of each week to see what's on the horizon, and what your boss's priorities are likely to be. Do they have a big meeting or conference coming up, for example? What can you do to help them prepare? Don't just assume that your boss will always be on top of everything – be their back-up. The better you get to know your boss, the more aware you'll be of what their weak spots are, and how best you can support them.

If a problem arises, don't just run straight to your boss expecting them to fix it (unless it's a really big, urgent problem, in which case they need to know as soon as possible!). Take a bit of time to think about how you would go about solving the problem, whether it's an unhappy customer, a deadline that has suddenly been shortened, or whatever. Always try to present your boss with a proposed solution to a problem: even if they decide to take a different course of action, they'll be grateful that you've tried to come up with an answer, rather than simply dumping the problem straight on to them.

On a similar note, don't be a moaner or complainer – stay positive and upbeat even if things are going pear-shaped. The last thing that a stressed-out manager needs to have to deal with is grumpy staff! Be someone that your boss is glad to have around.

Make your boss look good...

Consider one of the main purposes of your role as being an advocate for your boss. This is not as altruistic as it might sound. Your own visibility and progression are inseparably linked to that of your boss. If your manager is successful and respected within the organisation, that in turn will reflect on his or her team – including you. More specifically, your boss is likely to be appreciative of your support and respect, which will be very good for your working relationship.

But this isn't about being a creep. It's about making sure that you talk favourably and positively about your boss, both in public and private, and take opportunities to give praise where praise is due. It's about helping to cover up your boss's shortcomings – whatever they are. That doesn't mean lying for them, but it does mean doing what you can to help them portray themselves as positively as possible.

...But still get credit for your work

What do you do if your boss is one of those people who consistently takes the credit for your work? This is a tricky one! On the one hand, it's part of your job to make your boss look good. On the other hand, of course, it's going to be hard for you to progress if no one apart from your immediate line manager sees the quality of the work you do. Part of the solution is to make sure that you are taking action to build up your own profile. That could be something as simple as making sure that you copy your boss's boss into emails where a client has commended your work, for example.

Or you do what an ex-colleague of mine used to do, which was to initial all his work with an electronic footer showing his name, and protecting the document so that it couldn't be altered! Ultimately, if your boss is really not up to the job, and you or others are effectively covering for them, that is likely to come to light in due course. I would advise against making a huge issue out of it – your boss is the one person best placed to make your life difficult! If it's an ongoing problem, though, rather than just an occasional occurrence, then you should probably think about getting away from that particular boss – their actions will only hold you back.

REAL LIFE

Years ago, I was in charge of a team of researchers, most of whom were recent graduates and at the beginning of their careers. They were the brightest and most brilliant bunch of people I've ever worked with. What's more, they loved their jobs and were incredibly supportive of me as their manager – for instance, they wouldn't hesitate to work whatever hours were needed to get a job done. In return, their support was rewarded by my own loyalty to them: for example, if a customer ever had a reason to complain about a piece of research that one of my team had done, I would deal with the problem personally rather than pass the buck to the member of staff concerned. My team's loyalty to me meant that I was prepared to do everything I could to protect and support them.

Be loyal

I hope this goes without saying, but the main thing you owe your boss is loyalty. If your manager knows that you are trustworthy and supportive, they are much more likely to listen to you when something does go wrong, or to take your suggestions on board.

Getting the most out of your relationship

All of the advice above is focused – as it should be – on what you can do to support your boss. But how do you make sure that you, in turn, get the most out of your working relationship? Here are a few tips.

- **Ask for feedback.** Your boss might be one of those rare creatures who gives you frequent and immediate feedback on your work. But chances are your manager is more likely to rely on the organisation's formal appraisal system to comment on your performance – which could be as seldom as once a year. So make it your job to ask for feedback regularly – you don't want to get any shocks or surprises when appraisal time comes around. Instead, if you know where you're performing well and the areas your boss thinks you could improve on, you can take remedial action straightaway.

- **Don't be afraid to say 'no' – sometimes.** Your boss won't be fully aware of your workload unless you tell them about it. And most managers will keep piling work on to you until you squeal! It's your responsibility to let your boss know when you're overloaded – and it's their responsibility to decide what your priorities are in such a situation. Don't let them get away with saying that 'everything is a priority': if you really don't have time to complete both the tasks they've assigned you by the deadline they've given, then you need to get them to make a decision about what comes first. That's their job. (See Chapter 31 for more tips on how to say 'no' to your boss).

How to handle a nightmare boss

So much for how to handle your average boss. But what do you do if your manager is a real tyrant or dragon? I would say that it depends on how good they are at their job! If they are clearly successful and going places, brace yourself to deal with the difficult stuff and set out to learn as much as you can from them. If, however, they are widely disliked and disrespected in the organisation – get away from them as fast as you can! Their toxicity will taint you.

MAKING IT WORK IN PRACTICE

How to ask for a pay rise

Asking for a pay rise is one of the conversations that most people dread having with their boss. Here are a few tips to make it easier.

- *Do your research. What's the market rate for your job?*

- *Be ready to make your business case. Why do you deserve a pay rise? What value have you added to the organisation, or how have you saved it money?*

- *Schedule a meeting with your boss at a time when they are least likely to be distracted or interrupted.*

- *Make your case calmly and objectively. Don't ask for an answer there and then – give your boss time to think about it.*

- *Be prepared to compromise. If your boss says that there simply isn't any more money in the pot, could you negotiate some extra days' holiday, for example?*

- *If your boss tells you that a pay rise isn't justified, get them to be explicit about exactly what you would need to do to earn one.*

- *Never, ever try to call their bluff, for example by saying that you will leave if you don't get a pay rise. They might just take you up on it!*

IN A NUTSHELL

- Never underestimate the importance of your boss for your own career progression.

- Be supportive, loyal, positive and a problem-solver.

- Ask for regular feedback so that there are no surprises at appraisal time.

If you'd like to learn more about how to work well with your boss, I recommend:

Ros Jay, *How to Manage Your Boss: Or colleagues, or anybody else you need to develop a good and profitable relationship with,* Prentice Hall, 2002.

Don't be put off by the long title! This is a practical and very hands-on guide to managing other people, with the emphasis on how to manage your boss.

14

Be a team player

One of the best strategies you can adopt to help you shine at work is to become a great team player. Being able to work productively and collaboratively with others will have a positive effect on your own career.

It's not all about you

Excelling at work isn't about putting yourself before other people. In fact, one of the star qualities you should aim to develop is the ability to work brilliantly as part of a team. A collaborative, team-based approach will help you to build a reputation as someone who is trustworthy, considerate and unselfish – the kind of person we all want to work with.

Just as importantly, focusing on the needs of your team will help you to achieve more than you can achieve on your own. Being a great team player is a clever strategy for your own career.

How to be a team player

The guidelines for working effectively with your colleagues are pretty much the same as those for handling your boss: do what you can to make their job easier, be supportive and be trustworthy. In practical terms, this means sticking to the following rules.

- **Get to know your colleagues and how they like to work.** Everyone in the team will be different and have different strengths – and weaknesses. One person might be great at the 'big picture' stuff, for example, but less patient with detail. Someone else might be a brilliant communicator, but less of an ideas person. Understanding your colleagues' preferences and skills will help you to relate to them in the most effective way.

- **Be aware of other people's workloads, and be ready to help or lend a hand where you can.** That could be something as simple as making a cup of tea for someone who is stressing out over a deadline! Or it could be offering to help someone who's not as technologically savvy as you put together their PowerPoint presentation. Teamwork is about pitching in to help each other, so don't just sit there if other people are struggling – see what you can do to help.

- **Contribute**. Be someone who brings ideas to the team. Don't be scared to have an opinion – even if it differs from everyone else's. Teams work best when everyone plays their part – sometimes the best results come from a combination of different people's ideas, for example. It's not enough just to ensure that you carry out your own tasks well: if you're part of a team, then you share the responsibility for making sure that the whole team is on top of things.

- **Don't bitch, gossip or get involved in office politics**. Office politics can be such a minefield that I've devoted a whole chapter to it later (Chapter 17). But for now, just remember the golden rule that you shouldn't say behind anyone's back what you wouldn't be prepared to say to their face!

- **Stay positive, good-humoured and calm at all times – or as much as possible!** Don't blow problems out of proportion. Become known as the person who never flaps in a crisis. And be a friendly and fun person to be around!

MAKING IT WORK IN PRACTICE

Being a team player

Being a great team player really isn't rocket science. The bottom line is to treat people with respect and consideration. That doesn't mean that you need to treat everyone in the same way, though: get to know your colleagues and the best way to respond to them individually, and you'll quickly build a reputation as a brilliant team member.

Further strategies for being a team player

Maintaining these standards will make you someone that people are glad to have on their team. But, if you really want to build a reputation as a team player, there are broader and more strategic attitudes and approaches that you need to adopt. Let's look at these.

Be reliable and consistent

This might seem incredibly obvious, but you'd be surprised how many people manage – completely unintentionally – to irritate their colleagues by failing to follow some simple rules of work etiquette. There are few things more annoying than consistently having to 'cover' for colleagues who've forgotten an appointment, arrive late for a meeting, or don't deliver the work you've asked them for on time. It's the quickest way to lose 'brownie points', however good you are at your actual job. So make sure that you get the fundamentals right.

REAL LIFE

I once had a colleague, Alicia (in this instance, not her real name!), who was terrific at her job, but absolutely terrible at time management. At least once a week the office would get a call from someone whom she was supposed to be meeting, ringing to say that she hadn't appeared. It frustrated everyone in the office because, not only did dealing with the call waste our own time, but it made the whole firm look unprofessional. However good she was at her work, this kind of behaviour didn't do her reputation any good at all.

Work hard and get things done

Again, this point isn't exactly rocket science, but your colleagues will resent you enormously if they feel that you aren't pulling your weight. This isn't about getting into silly competitions about who stays latest in the office: it's simply about making sure that you are playing your full part as a member of the team, and not leaving other people to pick up your 'slack'. It's about being seen as a person who spends their work time working, not surfing the internet or taking endless personal calls. Build a reputation for taking your work seriously, doing what you do well and to deadline, and you'll become a valued and respected member of any team.

Share information

Team players are the people who recognise that the performance of the whole group is more important than their individual profile. Yes, if you are going to shine you need to build your own profile and reputation, but one of the best ways to do that is to be regarded as someone who is integral to the success of the team, not someone who is a 'loner' out only for their own advancement. So, be a sharer. Pass on information you glean about customers, clients or movements in the industry. Not only will this help you build your reputation as a team player, it will help you to gain respect as someone who is knowledgeable about the business and well-connected within it. Of course, there may be times when you need to make a judgement call about whether to pass on information that is given to you in confidence; but your general rule of thumb should be that you share the information you acquire, rather than hug it to yourself in the hope that it will give you some kind of advantage over your colleagues.

Don't go against the grain

In any team, there will always be instances where there is debate and disagreement about the right course of action. My advice is to go with the flow where possible, unless it's an ethical issue that you really don't feel comfortable with. Don't think that you will make your mark by disagreeing for disagreement's sake. You're more likely just to come across as a trouble-maker. Agreeing with the consensus view isn't a sign of weakness: it's a recognition that the collective view is often the best. Save your objections for instances where you fundamentally disagree on grounds of principle, or where you know that you have the experience and knowledge compellingly to present a different perspective.

Don't jump ship

Every team goes through periods of turbulence and difficulty. That might be because of market conditions (the industry is struggling and sales are hard to come by, for example), or because of internal issues (perhaps a new manager whom everyone finds it hard to work with). Whatever the reason, don't be the person who bails out first. If you want to demonstrate that you're a real team player, you have to be seen to put the needs of the team first. You need to be someone who is regarded as resilient in difficult circumstances, and who will go the extra mile to try to improve the situation.

Of course, if the future is looking really bleak, you must think about your own career strategy and what your options are, but don't bail out without doing – and being seen to do – everything you can to help fix the situation. The bond of loyalty that exists between colleagues who have worked together to weather a professional storm is an incredibly strong one, and will stand you in good stead whether you stay in your current organisation or ultimately move on somewhere else. You'll be remembered – and talked about – as someone who was professional and committed.

Working with difficult people

How do you handle a situation where you have to work with a really difficult colleague, or simply someone that you don't like? Chapter 21, on being influential, gives some more detailed advice on this thorny issue, but for now, remember a few golden rules.

- **Never rise to the bait**. However prickly or difficult your colleague is, treat them with courtesy and politeness at all times. Don't get involved in other people's complaints about them.

- **Don't give them any reason to criticise**. Make sure that your behaviour is impeccable at all times, and that you don't treat them differently than you do other people just because they're not as friendly or charismatic.

- **Don't take it personally**. The chances are that they are unfriendly or unpleasant to everyone. It's their problem, not yours. Don't dwell on it. If they're truly unbearable, do what you can to minimise your contact with them, but don't make a big issue out of it. You've got more important things to focus on.

IN A NUTSHELL

- Remember that 'no man is an island'. Mastering the art of being a strong team player will help you to make your mark at work.

- The fundamental rule is always to treat others with respect, and try to see things from their perspective.

- You can't be best friends with everyone at work, but you should aim to look for the best in people.

If you'd like to learn more about being a great team player, I recommend:
Stephen P Robbins, *The Truth About Managing People*, Pearson Education Ltd, 2008.

Comprehensive guide to managing behaviour in the workplace. As useful for team members as for managers.

15

Be a great manager

Management skills are one of the most sought-after – and hard to come by – skill sets in the work environment. Many people get promoted into management roles because they're good at their own job, but fail to appreciate the change that they have to make to be a manager. But building a reputation as a great manager from an early stage is a sure-fire way of boosting your profile and propelling your career forward.

Why management skills matter

In the last chapter, we looked at the behaviours and attitudes you need to adopt to be an effective team member. But at some point in your career, there's a pretty good chance that you'll end up managing a team of your own. This is one of the career 'hotspots' that can either enhance or ruin your reputation. Being good at your own job – and even being a great team player – is a completely different scenario from running your own team. That's because, as a manager, you're responsible for other people's performance and success, not just your own.

What makes a manager great?

What distinguishes a great manager from one who is merely competent – or, worse, wholly incompetent? Thousands of books have been written about the skills and behaviours required to be a good manager. The good news, however, is that the key principles of successful management can be distilled into a few golden rules. Not surprisingly, they are similar to the rules for working with your boss and your colleagues, although there are some additional attitudes and behaviours that you need to cultivate when you are given management responsibilities. For me, the following approaches form the basis of effective management:

- leading by example
- trusting and being trustworthy
- clarity
- consistency
- engagement.

Leading by example

In my opinion, your number one responsibility as a manager is to set a good example to your team. Your behaviour and attitudes will shape theirs. You can't afford to have a 'do as I say, not as I do' approach. If you regularly turn up late, miss deadlines or generally act in an unprofessional manner, you can't expect your team to act differently. The most effective way of getting your team to behave in a certain way is to behave that way yourself. That might sound obvious, but you'd be surprised how many managers regularly flout this basic rule. The bottom line is that your team will pay more attention to what you do than to what you say and will take their cues from your behaviour. Actions really do speak louder than words!

Trusting and being trustworthy

If you want your team to be motivated, confident and committed (and what manager doesn't?), you need to earn their trust. That means being open and honest, and acting with integrity. It means delivering on your promises, and acknowledging mistakes when you make them. Your team will forgive all sorts of other shortcomings so long as they believe that you are being straight with them and that you genuinely have their best interests at heart.

Equally, you must show that you trust your team. So, for example, don't delegate a task and then hover around micro-managing it. Recognise that other people have ways of working that may be different from yours, but are just as – or even more – effective. Be tolerant when people make mistakes – which they will. You actually have to give trust before it is earned: if you never give your staff the opportunity to demonstrate that they are trustworthy, you will never be able to be confident that they *are* trustworthy.

Clarity

Trusting your team to get on with things is not the same as failing to give them guidance. It is your responsibility as a manager to make sure that every member of your team understands their role, their responsibilities, and their contribution to the team goals. So you need to make those goals, and the actions needed to achieve them, crystal clear. Your team needs to know what your key priorities are, what outcomes you expect, and the timescales involved. That means that you need to communicate with them clearly and regularly; it also means that they must feel able to come to you with problems and ask for support when they need it.

> **TIP**
>
> *A good technique for ensuring clarity of purpose is the 'brief- back' approach: once you have briefed your team, or a team member, on a task, get them to repeat back to you their understanding of the task and the results that you are expecting. That way, you will minimise misunderstanding and ambiguity.*

Consistency

I've already stressed the need for consistency between your words and your actions, but there's more to it than that. A good manager will be consistent in how he or she treats their staff. That means not having favourites, and expecting the same standards of everyone. It also means making sure that your own approach is consistent. One of the most difficult scenarios for an employee to deal with is a manager who is chirpy and upbeat one day, and moody or snappy the next. Equally, it's incredibly frustrating and demoralising for your team if you aren't consistent about work standards.

There is a whole range of management styles, from autocratic through to collaborative, and they all have their advantages and disadvantages (although, where possible, collaborative is best), but the best advice I can give you on cultivating your management style is to be yourself, and be yourself consistently.

Engagement

A good manager cares about his or her team, and understands something about what 'makes them tick'. Get to know a bit about each of your staff. Where do they live? What is their partner called? Do they have children or pets? What do they enjoy doing outside work? What football team do they support? Building up a picture of the whole person, not just their work persona, will help you to understand what motivates and matters to them and make you better at managing them effectively.

15

Be a Great Manager

REAL LIFE

One of the best managers I ever worked for was a guy called Richard, who was my boss when I was in the Civil Service many years ago. Richard took the time to get to know all his staff, even down to the most junior members, and took a real interest in their work, however low-level it might be. As a result, he earned the complete and utter loyalty of everyone on his team. If Richard asked you to do something, nothing was too much trouble. His approach inspired everyone to give of their best. What's more, he made work a really fun place to be. He was my role model when I took on management positions myself.

Do inject a bit of fun into the office! Let your team know that it's ok to be human and relax a bit sometimes. There's more to work than just your pay cheque. But don't try to be 'one of the gang'. At the end of the day you are the boss, so you can never be best friends with your team. There will be times when they want to go for a drink without you. Don't fret about this, it's completely normal – they can't really let their hair down when the boss is there!

Handling mistakes

What happens if one of your team makes a mistake? In my view, it's really important in instances like this to distinguish between responsibility and accountability. Your team member may be *responsible* for the mistake (they sent out an email to the wrong client, for example), but it is you, as the manager, who is *accountable* for your team's performance. What that means in practice is that you should never, ever blame your staff as a way of defending yourself to more senior management. If they made a mistake, it's because you didn't train them properly, or didn't oversee the task in enough detail, or didn't make your expectations clear enough. You're the one who's paid to be the manager, and when mistakes occur, it's your job to step up to the mark. Your team – and your own managers – will respect you for it.

MAKING IT WORK IN PRACTICE

Management

Undertake regular '360 degree appraisals' with your team – this is where they get to give feedback on your performance. Even if it isn't current company policy, there's no reason why you can't introduce this kind of system for your own team. Explain to them that it's important to you to know their opinions, and you understand that it might be easier for them to be completely frank if the responses are anonymous: the best way to do this is by issuing a questionnaire that each of your team can complete and place in a specified place. Think of it as the management equivalent of a 'suggestion box'. What's important is that you find out how they really view you. That's the only way that you'll be able to sort out any little 'niggles' and keep improving your own performance.

IN A NUTSHELL

- Management is a serious responsibility. Good managers are trustworthy, consistent and lead by example.

- Great managers trust their teams. If you don't give people the opportunity to demonstrate that they are trustworthy, you'll never know that they are.

- Strong managers have the confidence to seek regular feedback from their team.

If you'd like to learn more about managing a team, I recommend:
Nic Peeling, *Brilliant Manager: What the best managers know, do and say,* Pearson Education Ltd, 2008.

A practical and honest guide to handling the challenges that most managers face.

16

Keep informed

You can never know too much! An enthusiastic and open-minded approach to your ongoing learning and development will help you to keep ahead of the game. People who like to learn are more interesting, more creative, and more successful than those who are happy to maintain the status quo.

The importance of learning

Your attitude to learning is key to your future employability. Employers want people who are well-informed, keenly aware of the world around them and able to spot opportunities. They want people who are comfortable with the latest technology, up-to-speed on current affairs, informed about the latest trends in business and management. Why? Because employees who are curious, keen to learn and widely-read are the ones who are most likely to succeed at work. If you're someone who's constantly trying to improve yourself, chances are you're someone who's constantly trying to do a better job at work. You're also someone who is interesting to be around!

But how do you use your desire to learn to shine? For me, the following actions are vital to help you harness the benefits of self-improvement.

Know your organisation

How well do you really know your company or organisation? Whether you're in marketing, finance, procurement, HR or any other role, you'll only be really effective if you understand how it contributes to the work of the organisation as a whole. This might sound pretty obvious – after all, you wouldn't dream of going for a job interview if you hadn't researched the company – you'd be surprised how many people operate in silos, carrying out their responsibilities as set out in their job description, without ever raising their head above the parapet to observe and learn about their company as a whole.

Why is this so important? Because it is the secret to being really, really good at your job. Too many people focus simply on the 'how' of their job – their day-to-day tasks, without thinking about the context within which they are operating. But if you take some time to think about the wider dimensions of your work – why you are actually doing it, and how it contributes to the company or organisation's ultimate goals – you'll find it much easier to identify your real priorities, and focus on the stuff that is truly important. And that will make you a much more effective employee.

Take every chance you can get to learn about other aspects of your organisation. Try the following.

- **Make it your business to read your company's mission statement, strategic plan, and annual reports**. If it all looks like gobbledy-gook (lots of mission statements do!), ask your manager to explain what it really means. You need to understand what your organisation is trying to achieve.

- **Jump at the opportunity to attend presentations or seminars by senior management**. The perspective of people higher up the organisation will be invaluable in helping you to work out what the real priorities are.

- **As a minimum, get to know as many people as possible in the organisation and take a real interest in what they do**. Think about how their work impacts on yours, and vice versa. How could you be more helpful to each other?

Know your sector, too

Don't just limit your learning to your own organisation. Find out about your competitors. What are they focusing on? What are the key challenges facing your sector? What's being said in the trade and business press about emerging trends and opportunities? This isn't industrial espionage, it's about being informed. Informed people make better decisions, whatever level they are working at.

At this stage you might find yourself thinking: 'But this isn't my role. We have strategy experts/management accountants/chief operating officers whose job it is to decide on the direction of the business'. While this may well be true, you will be much more effective – and impressive – in your own role if you have a genuine understanding of how it contributes to the overall agenda. And, you'll find it much more interesting!

Know what's going on in the world

Your understanding of the context you're operating in shouldn't just be limited to your own sector, either. There is a wide range of issues that will impact on your organisation's business, many of which will be outside its control, but will still need to be taken into account. You may well be familiar with the term 'PEST analysis' – an analysis of the political, economic, societal and technological factors that affect a company or sector. These four factors are a useful structure for raising your awareness of the context you are working in. I'm not saying that you have to become a political expert, an economics guru or a technology geek, but you should try to develop and maintain a broad understanding of the key areas that impact on your work. What legislative changes are in the offing that could affect the business you are in? What's happening in the world economy? What are the latest trends in buyer behaviour?

REAL LIFE

My friend James is one of the most widely-read – and interesting – people that I know. He keeps up-to-date on current affairs, financial issues, technology developments and popular culture. Not surprisingly, as a result of his wide-ranging and up-to-date knowledge he's also a very successful serial entrepreneur – constantly coming up with new ideas and opportunities. He's invariably the first person I turn to when I need a fresh perspective on my business.

Know a little about a lot

Knowledge of a wide range of issues will make you better at your job. It will give you perspective, prompt new ideas, and help to inform your work priorities. Not interested in politics? Well, you need to be. Politics underpins and drives everything that happens in the world. Our politicians make decisions that affect every aspect of our lives. You need to know who they are and what they're up to. Not interested in international affairs? You can't afford not to be. We live in a global world. What's happening in America, China and India will affect what's happening at home. Not interested in celebrity gossip? Fair enough! But you should know something about film, literature, theatre, music: cultural and consumer trends have an enormous impact on the world of business.

MAKING IT WORK IN PRACTICE

Keeping informed

You don't have to spend hours every day keeping up to speed with everything that's going on in the world – you don't have time. But you should try to keep abreast of key developments. Try the following.

- **Buy a newspaper every day and skim all the headlines.** *Don't be a creature of habit – try buying a different paper each day of the week. Keep yourself aware of what's going on and dip into issues here and there in a bit more depth.*

- **Use shortcuts.** *Sign up to a website that sends you a daily media summary. Subscribe to the* Economist *or* The Week *magazine, both of which provide good, succinct summaries of key news items on a weekly basis.*

- **Learn from other people.** *Seminars, workshops, even just conversation can all open up your mind to new ideas and thinking. Be a sponge – soak up knowledge from other people every chance you get.*

TIP

Make sure you always have some reading material with you. That way, whether you're stuck on a train, sitting in a waiting room, or waiting for your friend to show up for dinner, you've always got something to occupy you. Make the best use of your commute to work, too: if you go by train, read; if you drive, listen to the radio or a book on CD.

Know a lot about a little

We've now looked at why it's important to know a lot about your job, your company and your industry sector, but there are a few other areas where it's really good to be knowledgeable. In Chapter 4 we looked at how to carve out a niche for yourself by becoming an expert with skills that other people will value. Whatever else you choose to learn about in depth, don't neglect the following:

- **Learn about people, not just facts.** Knowledge is power, as they say, and knowledge about how people behave is the most powerful of all. You don't have to become an expert in psychology, but do expand your reading to include information about human behaviour. Understanding how other people are likely to behave in certain situations, how people make decisions, and what you need to know to get the best out of others, is information that will be invaluable to your career progression.

- **Get technology-savvy.** Technology has changed the way we work unrecognisably in just over a decade. It's hard to remember the days before email and the internet, yet they're pretty recent phenomena. If you're in the early stages of your career, you'll have grown up with technology. If you're older, it's something you'll have had to embrace. Either way, it pays to stay at the forefront of the technological revolution. Get comfortable with IT if you're not already. Learn how to use Excel, PowerPoint, the apps on your iPhone and any other up and coming form of technology. Understand the power of social media – it's the way forward. You can't afford to get left behind.

Finding learning opportunities

Don't rely on your employer to provide you with learning opportunities. Many good employers do offer all kinds of training to their staff – and if it's on offer, take advantage of it. But bear in mind that your learning and development is primarily your own responsibility. Be prepared to spend both time and money to expand your knowledge. Look on it as a long-term investment in your career. You have to be disciplined to carve out the time to expand your knowledge base, but it will always be time well spent. The broader your knowledge, the more valuable you will be as an employee – and the more options you potentially open up for yourself.

IN A NUTSHELL

• Work hard to really understand your organisation, both its written aims and objectives, and the unwritten rules.

• Keep on top of developments in your industry sector: be alert to threats and opportunities.

• Be aware of what's happening in the wider world: political, economic and technological changes can all impact on how you do your job and what your priorities should be.

• Take learning seriously. If you don't keep up to speed with what's happening around you, you'll get left behind.

17

Manage office politics

Office politics exists in every organisation, so you can't avoid it. The secret to managing it is to see it for what it is at its most basic level: using relationships and informal processes to help you get things done. It's about knowing who really holds the power and what the unspoken rules of behaviour are.

Office politics: is it so bad?

'Office politics' is a phrase that makes most of us shudder. Nearly every client I've worked with who has come to me for advice about changing their job or career has cited 'office politics' as one of the reasons why they want to leave. And yet, if it's something that everybody hates, why does anybody engage in it at all? The phrase conjures up images of backstabbing, bitching, manipulation, possibly even bullying. None of these things is pleasant or professional.

But you can argue that office politics gets a bit of a bad press. Another way of looking at it is to think of office politics as the informal channels through which things often get done, which can complement the more formal processes and systems in an organisation. For example, let's say you really need some face-to-face time with your boss, or your boss's boss, but his diary is always crammed full and it's hard to get to see him, but you have a really good relationship with his secretary. A quiet word with her, asking if there's anything she can do to help – and, hey presto, you've got your meeting. That isn't being manipulative, it's simply using your relationships and interpersonal skills to help you get what you need. Possibly without realising it, we all engage in this kind of 'politics' all the time. So, try to think of office politics as being about

REAL LIFE

I once worked in an office where the office manager – who was junior to the rest of us – delighted in making it clear when she was working on a 'confidential' project with the boss. I think it gave her some kind of power-trip. But it didn't make us think more highly of her – we just thought she was an insecure show-off, and when the results of the project, and the changes in our working pattern that it would entail, were finally 'unveiled', you won't be surprised to hear that they were met with lots of muttering, rolling of the eyes and not very much enthusiasm. If we'd all been involved at an earlier stage, and made to feel part of the project, we'd probably have responded a bit more positively.

relationship building and influencing, and you can see that it can be a force for good as well as evil!

Managing office politics

How do you manage the politics of the office to your advantage? Here are some pointers.

- **Understand who really holds the power in your organisation**. It's not always the person with the most impressive-sounding title! Be alert to who really seems to be 'in the know'. Who are the people that others most often turn to for advice or ideas? Who's really well-connected? These are the people that you want to cultivate your relationship with and get to know. And don't overlook the people who may not be in formal positions of authority, but who really do know most of what's going on – the security guard, the receptionist, even the cleaning lady are all people who have access to lots of information, and who get told all sorts of things by other people. Make them your friends.

- **Involve people sooner rather than later**. People don't like surprises, and they generally don't like to feel that something is being imposed on them. Resentment about not being involved in the development of changes that will impact on the way they work is one of the issues which can lead to cliques, backbiting and all the other negative aspects of office politics. So, if you're working on a project which is going to result in changes in the way your department does things, try to get people onside at an early stage. Consult them informally, ask their opinion, be open about what it is you're being asked to look into. Be as straightforward and consultative as you can. Nothing is guaranteed to wind people up more than if you appear to be hiding something.

- **Recognise that people have both professional and personal views**. Just because someone appears to be happy to go along with the boss's great new idea, it doesn't mean that they really think that – they're just trying to be professional, or don't want to be seen to 'rock the boat'. Use this to your advantage. Speak to people informally, have an 'off-the-record' conversation and ask them what they really think. If you're not in favour of whatever is being proposed, chances are you're not alone, but you won't win the argument if you don't have enough support. This isn't about trying to pit people against each other, but it's about recognising that people will not always give their true feelings away. Tapping into what's really going on in their minds will help you to understand their unspoken concerns – and help you to influence the outcome more effectively.

- **Make sure you understand the 'unspoken rules'**. It's not just about what's in the staff handbook. Be aware of how other people behave: what's acceptable and what isn't. Obeying the unspoken rules is the behaviour that will make you really 'fit in' and be one of the team. Often they're very simple protocols: for example, if you're making a cup of coffee for yourself, it's the done thing to ask if your immediate colleagues would like one too. Or it could be that everybody goes to the pub for a quick drink at lunchtime on Friday, but drinking at lunchtime isn't tolerated any other day of the week. Quite often these kinds of unwritten rules might not seem to have any particular logic: they're just habits and behaviours that have emerged over time. But ignore them at your peril.

- **Know what people like to be called**. Your boss might be known as Bill to his friends, William to his clients, and Mr Smith to anyone more junior than him. How you address someone says a lot about your relationship with them and your own standing in the organisation. Calling people by an abbreviation of their name that they haven't invited you to use is a sure way of rubbing them up the wrong way and inadvertently revealing that you don't really understand the rules of the game.

REAL LIFE

I once worked for a man called Gavin – a really great, friendly and approachable guy. One day, not long after I'd started in the role, I called him 'Gav' – mainly because everyone else in the organisation used one-syllable abbreviations of their name (so Catherine was known as 'Cath', Rachel as 'Rach' and so on). But Gavin was the boss and I hadn't realised that the same rule didn't apply! He very politely said to me: 'Jenny, my name's Gavin'. Lesson learned – but if I'd been more alert to how others in the office addressed him, I wouldn't have made the mistake in the first place.

Behaviour to avoid

So much for the positives. But there is a set of behaviours that give office politics its bad press, and you must avoid them at all costs. These behaviours include the following.

- **Gossiping, backstabbing and bitching**. For goodness' sake, you're not in the playground any more! Treat people the way you would like to be treated, and don't say anything behind anyone's back – or in an email – that you wouldn't be prepared to say to their face.

- **Taking sides**. Try to avoid getting pulled into other people's petty squabbles. Cultivate the art of being disinterested without being aloof. Be the 'neutral' person that other people turn to for real advice, not for back-up for their own personal agendas.

- **Blatant self-interest**. Of course you are the most important person in your universe, but don't put your personal goals and ambitions ahead of what is best for the team and the organisation. At least, don't be obvious about it!

- **Trying to win every argument.** You don't need to be 'right', or seen to be right, all the time. Choose your battles carefully. The last thing you want is to develop a reputation for being difficult or obstructive. If a change is being proposed, and it will really impact negatively on your workload or ability to do your job well, then it's worth doing all you can to make your case – and getting others to support you. But if it's no big deal, then don't make it into one.

IN A NUTSHELL

- Office politics is a normal part of working life – and it can be a good thing.

- Managing office politics is about understanding the informal rules and processes in your workplace – and using them to your advantage.

- There should be no space in your life for gossip, backbiting or self-promoting behaviour. That's what gives office politics such a bad name.

If you'd like to learn more about managing office politics, I recommend:
Richard Templar, *The Rules of Work*, Pearson Education Ltd, 2010.

A good general guide to workplace behaviour, with a strong emphasis on managing office politics.

18

Embrace change

In the world of work today, change is a given. You need to learn not just to handle it, but to embrace it. Periods of change at work can be 'hotspots' for your career: how you respond will be critical to your reputation and your future prospects. Understanding how to support people through periods of change – whether that's your boss or your team – is a skill set you need to learn.

Change happens

The one constant in the world of work today is change. The last decade has seen huge developments – in the fields of technology and communications in particular – that have brought enormous changes to working practices for most of us. It's hard to imagine that the internet is only a couple of decades old. Mobile phones, Blackberries, iPads and a host of other technology on offer mean that many of us can work just as effectively and efficiently outside the office as in it. Technology is increasingly blurring the boundaries between work and home life. And people who don't adapt to the new ways of doing things are going to be left behind.

The economic problems that the UK and the rest of the world faced recently are also going to have a huge impact on the working lives of many of us. The organisations and individuals who can prove themselves to be flexible, adaptable and nimble in the face of new financial and regulatory pressures will be the ones that survive and prosper. The ones who can't adapt to change will be the ones that go to the wall.

The lesson for anyone who wants to excel in the workplace is this: you need to be ready not just to deal with change, but proactively to embrace it. As human beings, we're often naturally resistant to change: most of us like the security of routine, at least some of the time. But if you're going to shine at work, you need to be a champion of change: someone who spots trends and stays at the forefront of developments, someone who is positive about the opportunities that change can bring.

Dealing with change

Many of the changes that you will have to deal with as you go through your career will be ones over which you have little or no control. That might be the arrival of a new boss, for example, or an organisational restructuring which changes the shape of your role or the team in which you work. But although you may not be in control of the circumstances themselves, you're always in control of how you respond to them. And it's vital to get your response right: changes such as a new manager or departmental structure can be career hotspots, and your reaction to them can make or break your career.

So, what's the best way to handle change? Here are the approaches that will mark you out as a winner.

- **Be prepared**. Handling change effectively is about minimising surprises as much as you can. In Chapter 16 we saw the importance of understanding the context within which you're working. Are there legislative changes in the offing that will affect the way you or your organisation have to work? Is the economic situation likely to lead to restructuring or redundancies? Being able to spot what's over the horizon will help you plan how you're going to cope with changes, and ensure that you're ready for them. Identifying potential threats or changes at an early stage means you have more time to plan your response and to stay one step ahead, whether that means altering the way in which you work, or starting to look for new career opportunities if your sector or company is struggling. Fore-warned is fore-armed, as they say.

- **Get involved**. If your department or organisation is planning major changes, they may well undertake some kind of consultation exercise. Make sure you play your part in this if you get the opportunity: there's no point in moaning about changes you're not happy with after the event, if you didn't speak up at the time! If there's no formal consultation, and your boss or company has simply announced big changes, find an opportunity to talk to your boss informally about them. Chances are your manager is just as unsettled as you might be feeling, so be supportive. Find out what you can about what the consequences are likely to be, but let your boss know that you'll do what you can to make their life easier.

- **Be positive**. Change is often stressful, and many people's instinctive reaction is to be negative and resistant. Don't let that be your reaction. You don't have to gush with enthusiasm you don't really feel, of course, but if your thoughts are negative, it's best to keep them to yourself. Be measured, reasonable and, as I've said above, be as supportive as you can.

MAKING IT WORK IN PRACTICE

Handling change

Don't waste your time and energy fretting or complaining about changes that you can't influence or control. Far better to focus on how you are going to deal with the new situation, and how you can make the best of it, whether that's a new boss, an internal restructuring, or even the threat of redundancy.

Of course, not all change is for the worse! There could be a promotion on the cards for you, or a chance to take on new and wider responsibilities. Again, your approach should be positive: even if you're nervous about what's being offered, don't let it show. If senior people in the organisation think that you're reluctant to step up to the mark, that will affect their level of confidence in you. Be up for a challenge.

> **TIP**
>
> *You should also bear in mind that new opportunities for you might mean that one of your colleagues misses out, so, even if you're really excited by the changes being proposed, don't go overboard. Read the mood of the office and be sensitive to other people's responses.*

Managing change

What about a situation where you are responsible for initiating change? Perhaps your boss has asked you to manage a new project that will affect not only your workload and priorities, but those of your colleagues or team. Or maybe you yourself have identified some different ways of working that you think will make your team more effective. How do you get – and keep – your colleagues on board? Keep the following in mind.

- **Know what you want to change – and why**. Before you start to involve other people, make sure that you are very clear about the changes you are proposing – and why they are necessary. If you're going to bring other people along with you, you'll need a strong and convincing business case.

- **Get people involved**. The number one rule about introducing change is: don't take people by surprise if you can possibly help it. If changes are on the card, seek to involve your team from the earliest possible stage. Canvass their ideas: as we saw in the last chapter, people are less likely to resist change if they feel they have been able to influence decisions, at least to some extent. If it's a change that's being imposed on you, and you have absolutely no wriggle-room, then communication is even more important. Keep your team up-to-date with developments, and allow them plenty of opportunity to ask questions. Don't dismiss their concerns, but seek to allay them where you can.

- **Understand people's resistance**. Resistance to change is a natural response. Even if the changes are clearly sensible, there may well be people in your team who don't respond enthusiastically. Be understanding of this: people take time to get used to change. Whatever your own reservations, don't voice them in front of your team. Look for the positives. But give people an opportunity to voice their concerns and 'get it off their chest'. Far better for discontent among your team to be out in the open, rather than have people simmering with resentment behind your back.

- **Be as consistent as you can in other areas**. We've already seen that consistent behaviour is one of the hallmarks of a good manager. This is especially important in times of change. As a manager, you need to maintain a positive and measured approach, however stressed or discontented you yourself may be feeling. So if there are big changes afoot try to keep your behaviour and working methods as normal as possible to help alleviate any worries people may have.

- **Avoid change for change's sake.** Of course you need to keep your eyes open for new opportunities, new trends and new ways of working, but there is nothing more disconcerting for your team than a constant flow of new initiatives, launched with pizazz and then allowed to fizzle out when a new project becomes flavour of the month. Your team will have a limited level of tolerance for change: don't use up their vital goodwill on changes that really aren't necessary.

REAL LIFE

I once worked for a boss who was a real 'flitter'. Almost every week without fail, he would produce a new proposal or a fresh set of priorities for us to work on. Unsurprisingly, it didn't take us long to come to the conclusion that there was little point in putting effort into any of his new ideas, as we could almost certainly predict that they'd be abandoned in a week or two in favour of some other 'priority'. Like the boy who cried 'wolf', it meant that even when the boss did try to introduce something that could be both useful and sustainable, we found it pretty hard to summon up much enthusiasm.

IN A NUTSHELL

- Being able to respond positively to changes in the workplace will mark you out as someone who is flexible, adaptable and up for it.

- Remember that change can be a positive thing, both for your organisation and your own career. Look for the upsides and the opportunities.

- Understand many people's resistance to change, and make it as comfortable a process as you can for them.

If you'd like to learn more about managing change, I recommend: Michael Fullan, *The Six Secrets of Change: What the best leaders do to help their organizations Thrive and Survive,* Jossey Bass, 2008.

A fascinating study of change in the workplace. The writing style is quite 'academic', but worth persevering with!

19

Improve your thinking

Improving the quality of your thinking will help you to deal better with business planning, problem-solving and decision-making. Each of us has our own preferred way of thinking, but working to develop a range of thinking skills will help you to perform at your best in every situation.

Think about how you think

To a large extent, your success at work is dependent on your thinking ability. The further you progress in your career, particularly if you are following the 'upwards' route, the more likely it is that you will encounter uncertainty, complexity and unpredictability. Towards the bottom of an organisation you are likely to find rules, processes and direct reporting lines. The closer you get to the top, however, the more risk, fluidity and change you will have to manage. These are the kinds of situation where you need top-class thinking skills.

Each of us has our own natural 'thinking disposition': some people are great at 'blue skies' or 'big picture' thinking – they quickly see the context within which a decision has to be made, for example. Others are good at logical thinking: working out the best order in which to tackle a series of tasks, perhaps. Still others are strong 'critical thinkers': spotting the right questions to ask, and drilling right down into the issue.

The key to strong thinking is to be able to apply different types of thought to different situations, according to what's appropriate. For example, there will be times when you need broad thinking skills – to be able to make new connections and push boundaries. In another situation, you might require strategic thinking – to identify your objectives and plans.

The good news is that the quality of our thinking has nothing to do with our innate intelligence. We can teach ourselves to think more effectively. How? The first step is to be aware of your default thinking disposition – the way in which you naturally tend to think about things. Then you can become aware, and start to make use of, different thinking tactics, according to the situation you're in or the problem you're facing. Let's look at some of the most important approaches.

Strategic thinking

Strategic thinking is about a focus on the longer-term. Strategic thinkers focus on missions, objectives and goals. They're clear about what they're trying to achieve, and why, even if they haven't yet worked out the detail of how they're going to get there. Indeed, strategic thinkers often like to leave the detail of implementation to others: they prefer the 'big picture'. So, how can you make your thinking more strategic?

- As ever, be aware of context. What's happening in your sector or your organisation that could present threats or opportunities, or require you to adapt what you're doing?

- Get clear about exactly what you're trying to achieve. What's the purpose of your role? What are your specific objectives? What's your approach (or strategy) for getting there?

- How will you measure your (or your team's) success?

Critical thinking

Critical thinkers are the people who seek out and analyse information, look for evidence rather than opinion and question other people's assumptions. Their thinking is rational and knowledge-based. Sometimes they can appear overly cautious about the conclusions that they are prepared to draw from the information available. The value of critical thinkers is that they are often the people who will spot the underlying flaw in a proposal, which more strategic or creative thinkers might be more ready to gloss over. To improve your critical thinking try the following techniques.

- **Don't rely on second-hand sources or 'accepted wisdom'.** Discipline yourself to check the reliability and objectivity of information (for example, has the report that you're going to base your presentation on been written by someone with a particular policy axe to grind?).

- **Don't let your thinking or decision-making get sloppy.** Get the information you need to inform your decision. Evaluate the information you have, and get into the habit of listing pros and cons of different actions.

- **Be aware of where you are making assumptions that aren't – or can't be – backed up by evidence.** That doesn't mean that you should never make assumptions, but just be clear about when you are doing so – and make it clear to others.

Relational thinking

Relational thinkers are the people whose working style is inclusive and collaborative, who instinctively look for a 'win-win' solution to problems. They tend to regard their work as more about relationships than transactions, and will put strong emphasis on issues such as trust and quality of service. Relational thinkers will instinctively take account of the 'human' side of work projects and problems, such as the effect on staff wellbeing or the level of customer service. They're usually strong team players and often make great managers. How can you improve your relational thinking?

- **Focus on your listening skills.** In meetings, for example, discipline yourself to concentrate fully on what the speaker is saying, rather than planning what you are going to say next. (See the next chapter for more on listening skills).

- **Train yourself to think about other people's perspectives.** If you're putting together a business proposal or working on a project, for example, try to anticipate your clients' or colleagues' likely response. What might they criticise or be concerned about?

- **Think 'win-win'.** What's the best solution not just for you, but for the others involved?

REAL LIFE

I would say that I am naturally a 'relational' thinker, but over the years I've had to develop a range of other thinking approaches. For example, as a fast-stream civil servant working on the development of criminal justice policy, critical thinking skills were key, while strategic and creative thinking were what was needed when I set up my own business. I've learned to adjust my thinking style to suit the situation that I'm in. Identify the type of thinker you are but make sure you also know how to adjust your thinking style to adapt to different situations.

Creative thinking

Of all the different thinking styles, creative thinking is the one that many people find difficult. One of the things that I most often hear clients say when we are talking about their skill set is: 'I'm not creative'. I think that's because, too often, we have a pretty narrow definition in our minds of what constitutes creativity. Usually, people are thinking of 'creativity' in terms of the arts: writing, painting or design, for example. But creativity can be defined much more broadly: put simply, being 'creative' means seeing something from a new angle or finding a different way of doing something. Whether you're good at advising friends on their relationship problems, planning and organising a social event, or simply making a tasty meal out of whatever leftovers are lurking in the fridge – you're being creative.

So why do so many of us struggle to be 'creative'? Perhaps one of the biggest hurdles is our tendency to think that if a problem could be solved, it would have been solved already. Surely there's someone out there who is cleverer or more knowledgeable than we are, who would have found a better way of doing something, if that were possible? Not necessarily! I read recently that innovations in industry almost always come from individuals outside of the area of the invention. Perhaps people working in the industry are too close to their product to see an alternative application for it or an 'obvious' way of improving it.

Other blocks to creativity include the assumption that there is only one solution or 'right' answer or way of doing things; the assumption that a 'creative' solution has to be complex; and that you can't force creativity – you either have an idea or you don't. This last point is probably the most misleading of all. The fact is that you can apply a variety of techniques to help you generate ideas. These range from thinking about how you could tweak or 'evolve' existing systems and processes, through to using tools such as brainstorming and mind-mapping to help you come up with 'revolutionary' ideas. The key thing to remember is that we don't usually have ideas just for the sake of it – no one sits down and says 'right, I've got a blank sheet of paper, and I'm going to have an *idea!'* We have ideas because we have problems to solve: the problem itself is our starting point for creativity.

What can you do to boost your creative thinking?

- **Start by recognising the ways in which you are already creative:** perhaps you are great at making up recipes from scratch, or you're really good at caption competitions, or have a flair for writing great copy. Acknowledging your existing creative streak is a great way of boosting your self-confidence in your ability to be creative in other areas, including at work.

- **Feed yourself with information:** the more you learn, the more widely you read and the more people you talk to, the more likely it is that you will come up with new ideas and approaches.

- **Mix things up a bit. Change your routine:** take a different route to work, go somewhere new for lunch, buy a book on the bestseller list that you wouldn't normally read. Observing and doing new things wakens up your mind and helps you think in fresh ways.

MAKING IT WORK IN PRACTICE

Creative thinking

Make notes of the ideas or issues that interest you – perhaps stories that you read in newspapers, or an article that you come across in a magazine or on-line. Keep your notes all together in one place and review them every couple of weeks or so. This is a great way of making mental connections you hadn't thought of before and coming up with new approaches.

IN A NUTSHELL

• Think about how you think. Be aware of your default thinking approach: it won't always be the most appropriate way of approaching a problem.

• Different situations require different thinking processes. Work to develop not just your thinking styles, but your awareness of which kinds of situation each is best suited to.

• Key thinking styles that you should cultivate are strategic thinking, critical thinking, relational thinking and creative thinking.

If you'd like to learn more about improving your thinking, I recommend:
Edward de Bono, *Teach Yourself to Think*, Penguin, 1996.

This is the 'bible' of books on thinking, with a particular slant towards problem-solving. Highly recommended.

20

Communicate brilliantly

Good business relationships are based on communication. The key skills of a good communicator are being able to listen properly and being able to get your own message across logically, succinctly – and compellingly. Each of these skills relies on the ability to empathise and to build rapport.

The importance of communication

The ability to communicate effectively is one of the most important skill sets for a successful career. Along with relationship management skills, they form the basis of success at work. Why? Because, ultimately, all business and work boils down to these two elements: communicating a message and managing relationships with people. It doesn't matter how knowledgeable, or creative, or strategic you are, if you can't get your point across to people and get them on board, you're going nowhere!

Listening skills

When you read the word 'communication', what do you think of? Chances are the image in your mind is a proactive one, like giving a presentation or talking to your team. In fact, the basis of successful communication is the skill that we tend to regard as passive rather than active – or that maybe we don't even think of as a skill at all – the ability to listen.

Why are listening skills so important? Firstly, listening allows you to understand the context you are operating in. Whether that's something as simple as sensing the mood of the person you are speaking to, or something more complicated, such as getting to the heart of what your client's problem really is, the ability to listen intelligently helps you to fully appreciate the situation before you respond. Secondly, listening helps you to build up rapport. A genuine interest in what the other person is saying is the most effective way of establishing a good relationship. Finally, listening helps you to tailor your message to suit the recipient. As well as fully understanding the viewpoint of the other person, being aware of their body language, and their tone and pace of voice, can help you to respond to and communicate with them much more effectively.

So, how do we improve our ability to listen? Here are some pointers.

- **Maintain eye contact**. Not in a mad, staring kind of way, of course! But keeping your attention visually focused on the person who is talking to you will help you to concentrate on what they are saying.

- **Make a real effort to focus fully on what the other person is saying**. If it helps, paraphrase in your mind the points they are making. The key things to avoid are 1. interrupting the other person, either to finish their sentence or, worse, with an anecdote of your own and 2. thinking about what you are going to say in response to them while they are still talking.

- **Try to listen with complete concentration – your chance to respond will come**. Be warned: this is really difficult! But it gets easier with practice, and it's a skill well worth mastering.

- **Look for the visual messages as well as just hearing what is said**. Often a person's real reaction can be spotted in their body language rather than their words.

Every conversation is a presentation

'Presentation' is a word that strikes fear into the heart of even the most apparently confident people. If that's how you feel, I'm afraid I have some bad news for you: presentation skills are critical to your career progression. But there's good news too: anyone can learn to be an effective presenter, as long as they make use of two tools: preparation and practice.

We tend to think of 'presenting' as addressing an audience in a formal setting. But I'd like you to think of it this way: every time you are speaking in a work context, you are presenting. You might be explaining the requirements of a project to your team, or updating your boss on progress on a piece of work, or even asking them for a pay rise! Whenever you are in a situation where you are trying to get a message across – you are presenting. A formal presentation to a large audience is simply one – albeit advanced – form of presentation, and the same basic rules apply whether you are speaking to one person or 100. So let's look at the key principles of successful presenting, whatever the size of your audience.

- **Preparation is everything.** A presentation can be bad for many reasons: it may be that the speaker is nervous or the acoustics are poor, for example. But in my experience the most common reason for a bad presentation is that the speaker clearly hasn't prepared properly. Whatever the size of your audience, or however informal the meeting, it's criminal not to be properly prepared.

- **Understand the context.** Be clear about who your audience is, why you are addressing them, and what their expectations are. What do they want to learn from what you have to say? Also, it's important to be aware of any recent developments, whether internal or external, that could have an impact on what you are going to say or even on the mood of the audience.

- **Be very clear about the key points you want to make.** Keep the structure simple. If you try to pack too much in you'll just confuse the listener. A good structure, regardless of whether you are in an informal situation with a few people, or a more formal one with a big audience, is to start off by stating your key point, proceed to give the information that backs it up, and finish by repeating that key point.

- **Keep it brief.** Being able to make your point clearly and concisely is a sign that you have thought about what you want to say in advance, and considered the best way of saying it. Most people's attention span is pretty short, so don't give your audience an excuse to 'switch off'. Even if you're speaking in a formal environment – at a conference, for example – where you've been given a specific time slot, it's a good idea to make sure that your presentation won't take up all of the allotted time. Organisers hate nothing more than the speaker who over-runs and messes up the rest of the schedule! So err on the side of brevity – if need be, you can always take questions at the end to fill the remaining time. Trust me, no one in the audience is going to resent the fact that you finished a bit early!

- **Know your material inside out.** That way, even if you lose your place in your notes, you won't be stuck because you'll be able to remember what comes next.

- **Focus on your voice.** Practise changing pace, lowering and raising your tone of voice, and so on – just as you would in normal conversation. There's nothing worse than listening to monotone.

REAL LIFE

A number of years ago I was invited to give a presentation on 'developing your career' to a large group of telecoms professionals. It didn't go well: I couldn't seem to build up any rapport with the audience – it was hard to find even one friendly face! In short, I bombed. It was only a few days later, when I found out that around a third of my audience had just been told that they were to be made redundant, that I understood why they hadn't exactly been receptive to what I had to say. If only someone had thought to update me on the context… So the moral of the story is: make sure you know as much as possible about your audience and their circumstances!

MAKING IT WORK IN PRACTICE

Communication

Take any opportunity you can to get feedback on your presentational style – painful as it may be at the time, it's the surest way of helping you to improve quickly. Whether you've addressed an informal team meeting, or a much larger audience, seek out a few people whose opinion you trust and ask them what they really thought of what you said and how you said it. Use their feedback to help you do even better next time.

IN A NUTSHELL

- Communication skills are the bedrock of business success. Understanding other people's perspective and being able to get your own message across clearly are critical abilities.

- Listening is the most important communication skill of all. Learning to listen well will allow you to pick up on nuances and underlying messages, and tailor your own message to the audience.

- Every time you have a conversation in a work environment, you are presenting. Being absolutely clear about your message is the key to successful presentation.

If you'd like to learn more about communicating brilliantly, I recommend:
Richard Hall, *Brilliant Presentation: What the best presenters know, do and say*, Pearson Education Ltd, 2008.

A clear and simple guide to presenting to both large and small audiences.

21

Be influential

Influence is the art of bringing people round to your way of thinking. Logic, empathy and a collaborative approach will help you to be persuasive. How you conduct yourself professionally and the level of respect that people afford you are also key factors in increasing your sphere of influence. In other words, being influential is an ongoing process, not a one-off event.

Influencing: winning hearts and minds

We use influencing – or negotiating – skills in all areas of our life, often without being particularly conscious of it! Whether you're trying to persuade your partner to go out for dinner instead of cooking, or making the case to your boss for a promotion or pay rise, what you're really trying to do is to get them to see things your way. As your career progresses, you're increasingly likely to find yourself in situations where you are not simply presenting information, but are actively seeking to influence people's thinking and persuade them to your preferred course of action.

The essence of successful influencing is bringing people around to your way of thinking. It's not about coercion – except, perhaps, in a crisis situation where a decision needs to be made quickly and there's no time for discussion. In any case, in many situations you will find yourself trying to influence sideways or upwards (ie people who are your peers or even who are senior to you), so coercion isn't an option. Instead, you need to be able to persuade them that your approach is the best one.

Sometimes clear presentation of a logical and compelling argument might be enough to persuade others. But in many cases, you'll find that you need to win over not just people's minds, but their hearts: in other words, you need to persuade them not just that they *should* do something, but that they actually *want* to do it. How do you do that? Here are the golden rules: it shouldn't surprise you that I've touched on some of them in the previous chapter – that's because key elements of successful influencing are listening and presenting well.

- **Be clear about what you are trying to achieve.** What is the outcome you are seeking? Can you make your case clearly, logically and succinctly? Can you anticipate what the other party's objections might be and, if so, what is your response?

- **Avoid exaggerating your case, or making use of definitive statements when in fact you are merely**

voicing your own opinion. Be rational, objective and professional at all times. Don't use forcing statements like 'you must' or 'you should'. Instead, make it clear that you are presenting your own point of view, as a basis for discussion.

- **Try to see the situation from the other person's perspective, not just your own**. Put yourself in their shoes, and listen properly to their responses to what you are saying. What are they really concerned about?

- **Think in terms of co-operation, not competition**. The ideal outcome of any discussion is a 'win-win' situation, where both parties walk away content. There are very few situations where your position and that of the person you are seeking to persuade will be mutually exclusive. Is there a compromise that you can reach that you will both be happy with? Compromise isn't a sign of weakness or lack of assertiveness; it's a grown-up attitude which shows that you understand and care about the other person's perspective and needs. People will be far more willing to meet you halfway (or more) if they feel listened to, understood and appreciated.

MAKING IT WORK IN PRACTICE

Influencing

Being a successful influencer doesn't mean that you have to 'win' or 'be right' all the time. If you're prepared to compromise on issues that ultimately aren't that important to you, you're storing up some emotional and business capital for those occasions when you really do feel strongly about an issue. That said, however strongly you feel about something, never lose sight of the fact that, in the long-term, your relationship with the person you are seeking to influence is probably more important than the outcome of one particular debate. Be gracious, flexible and collaborative, and your sphere of influence will grow.

Influence isn't just a one-off performance

The points above are aimed at situations where you want to get agreement to a specific course of action: the go-ahead for a project, for example, or an increase in your budget. But being truly influential goes deeper – and wider – than the ability to persuade others to your course of action. Real influence is when other people proactively seek out your opinion and advice, on different occasions, because they respect your knowledge and your judgement. Your level of influence grows with your professional reputation.

Influencing difficult people

However strong your interpersonal and influencing skills are, at some point in your career you are bound to come across people who are difficult to deal with. In my experience, the most difficult people fall into three categories: negative, contrary and downright nasty. How do you handle people like that?

The negative person

Some people's default setting seems to be 'no', where they can only say things like 'that will never work' or 'we've never done it like that before'. However they phrase it, they like to put the dampeners on everything. Their negativity might stem from insecurity or fear of change, or they might have been around for a while and simply feel that they have seen it all before. Whatever their reasons, what's the best way to deal with them? Here are my top tips.

- **Don't rely on your interpersonal skills to win them over.** The only chance you have of getting them onside is to demonstrate the benefits – to them – of what you are proposing.

- **Give them facts, figures and information**. Make the business case for your proposal.

- **Anticipate their likely objections and have your responses ready**. Be factual, clinical and concise.

The contrary person

Some people seem to take a positive delight in being contrary or antagonistic. Perhaps they think that they know best, or maybe they just simply enjoy being the person who can come up with objections or throw a spanner in the works. This kind of behaviour can stem from insecurity, arrogance, jealousy – or all of these!

REAL LIFE

Some time ago, I worked with a senior manager who was exactly this type of contrary person. Everything I suggested, he opposed. Everything I said, he tried to undermine. I think he thought I was simply a young 'whippersnapper' and resented the fact that I had been appointed to a senior (and well-paid) position. Or maybe he was just difficult from birth! So how did I deal with this person? I followed the tips outlined below.

How do you deal with this kind of contrary behaviour?

- **Don't take it personally**. Chances are they treat everyone else like this too.

- **Do what you can to 'neutralise' them**. Don't involve them in decisions that you don't have to. Work around them where possible.

- **When you do have to involve them, employ your charm**. Compliment them (sincerely). Let them know you respect their opinion, but be prepared to be assertive and stick to your guns.

The nasty person

Thankfully, there really aren't too many of them around, but most of us at some point in our career will come up against a colleague who is difficult to work with, simply because they are downright unpleasant. Perhaps they're just unfriendly, but they might also be openly rude, sarcastic or argumentative. So what's the best way to handle someone like this?

- **Be pleasant and polite at all times.** Even the rudest person will find it difficult to maintain that stance in the face of constant charm!

- **Don't allow yourself to get stressed by the situation.** It's highly unlikely that you're the only person they're being unpleasant towards.

- **Keep it in perspective.** Give them as wide a berth as you can, and remember that people only treat other people badly because for some reason they feel bad about themselves. So be understanding if you can!

REAL LIFE

Years ago, I worked with a lady called Sylvia. She was the most singularly unpleasant person I have ever come across! Her approach was abrupt to the point of rudeness, she never missed an opportunity for a sarcastic or withering comment, and she treated everyone around her like fools. She wasn't my boss (thank goodness), but she was senior to me, and I figured that it was in my best interests to try to get her on side as far as possible. I adopted the 'charm offensive' approach: saying good morning, bringing her a cup of coffee now and again, always being courteous regardless of how rude she herself was being. I can't say that any of this resulted in a personality change on her part, but she definitely thawed a little. And, if I'm honest, I got quite a lot of pleasure out of feeling that I was on the moral high ground!

IN A NUTSHELL

- Successful influencing relies on the ability to listen effectively and to present your own point well. The most influential approaches are collaborative, not competitive.

- How you act on a day-to-day basis – not just on key occasions – is what ultimately determines your professional reputation, and therefore your level of influence.

- Some people will always be difficult to handle. Recognise their behaviour for what it is and don't take it personally.

If you'd like to learn more about influencing, I recommend:
James Borg, *Persuasion: The art of influencing people,* Pearson Education Ltd, 2004.

A straightforward, easy and highly practical read, enhanced with lots of humorous examples.

22

Be decisive

Effective decision-making is a key business and career management skill – and the more your career progresses, the more likely you are to find yourself having to make decisions in situations that are complex, uncertain and require the exercise of judgement. A key skill is being able to identify which decisions require a lot of attention, and which ones are of less consequence – and to apply your time and thought appropriately.

Am I indecisive – or not?

It's a bit of a myth that people are either 'decisive' or 'indecisive': the fact is that each of us will have times when we can make a decision quickly, and other times when we find ourselves pondering for a long time and feel unable to come to a conclusion. Your degree of confidence in making a decision can depend on the importance you attach to it ('this is a big decision and I need to get it right'), how much you know about the issue ('I don't know enough about this'), or the range of choices available to you ('there are just too many options to choose from'). So how can you help yourself avoid those feelings of indecision? Here are my tips for good decision-making.

Decide which decisions are important

We can waste an awful lot of time at work trying to make a decision about something that ultimately probably isn't very important. The key to good decision-making is to be able to recognise when a decision is likely to have significant implications – and therefore needs to be carefully thought through – and where the outcome of whatever decision you make probably won't matter that much in the long run. So your starting point for any decision should be to ask yourself 'How much does this really matter?'

A good approach here is to answer the question 'How much will this matter in a week/month/year?' If the answer is that it won't matter at all in a week or a month, then don't waste too much time on the decision – save your time and energy for the big stuff.

Straightforward decisions

In any one day at work, you're likely to find yourself having to make lots of different decisions. In fact, you're probably not aware of quite how much time you spend on decision-making, because many of the choices you make will be so straightforward that they are almost automatic. Clear your emails first or return phone calls? Stay late in the office or go to the networking event? You usually make decisions at this level on a fairly instinctive basis, and that's absolutely fine.

Get into the habit of making straightforward decisions quickly. Put a time limit on your decision-making. Don't use decisions as an excuse to procrastinate: the time you spend trying to make up your mind is time that could probably be spent more productively getting on with implementing your decision!

Making big decisions

What's the best approach when you're faced with a much bigger decision? Maybe you have to decide where to make budget cuts for your department, for example, or whether to accept a promotion that you've been offered. Here are some ways to make the decision less daunting.

- **Be clear about what you are actually trying to achieve**. Take the budget cuts example: think about the priorities for your or your team's role. What could you afford to do less of without compromising your overall output? What will your and your team's success be measured on at the end of the year? Put your decision in the context of the medium to longer-term.

- **Make sure you are in possession of all the facts – or as many as possible**. The best decisions are made from a position of knowledge, not based on whim or perception. That doesn't mean that you won't ultimately need to make a 'judgement call', but it's much easier to do this – and to defend your decision subsequently – if you can articulate a fact-based rationale for your choice.

- **Assess all your options – then narrow them down**. Research carried out by the eminent psychologist Barry Schwartz found that people tend to get paralysed when they have too many options. In his research, he surveyed customers making a decision about which jam to buy in a supermarket. Where there were only half a dozen jams to choose from, buyers found the decision easy but, where there were more than 20, many found it hard to make a decision at all. So, eliminate as many options as you can relatively quickly, and focus on the two or three 'front-runners'.

- **Figure out what type of decision you need to make.** Decide whether this decision needs to be a 'maximiser' – the best decision, or whether being a 'satisficer' will do – a 'good enough' decision. In many instances, there will be more than one solution, each of which may work perfectly well.

- **Use the 'balance sheet' method.** Sum up the pros and cons of your different choices. Write down the advantages and disadvantages of each possible course of action and its likely consequences. It's useful to try to put the pros and cons in some order of priority, so that you give more weight to the most important factors.

- **Use other people as a sounding-board.** Don't be tempted to ask too many people, but be aware of limiting your consultation to people whom you think are most likely to agree with your own instinct. It's good to get, and take account of, differing opinions. You should also beware of group-think: research suggests that groups can often make more 'risky' decisions than individuals, because no one person feels responsible. If the outcome is ultimately your responsibility, you need to make sure that you are fully comfortable with the decision you make, regardless of the pressure from others.

- **Mull things over.** Put the issue to one side for a while and focus on something else. If it's a really big decision, chances are you have a bit of time to come up with your plan of action.

- **Test yourself.** If, having analysed all the facts at your disposal, you're still struggling to decide between two options, here's a good little trick: allocate one option as 'heads' and the other as 'tails' and spin a coin. How do you feel if the 'heads' option comes up? Relieved? Slightly disappointed? Do you secretly wish that 'tails' had come up instead? This technique is a good way of harnessing your gut instinct – in the absence of any strong factors to sway your decision, it's your instinct that you'll need to rely on. Don't be afraid of this – providing you've got your facts right, you're unlikely to be too far off the mark whichever judgement call you make.

MAKING IT WORK IN PRACTICE

Being decisive

Focus on a decision that you have to make in the near future, whether it's a work-based one, or something personal such as where you're going to go on holiday. How would you normally approach this decision? Which of the tools or techniques listed above could you use to help you make a better decision? Make a note of how exactly you reached your conclusion. Then re-visit your decision in a month's time – was it a good decision? Think about what was different about how you made your choice, and how you can utilise that approach in relation to future decisions.

You won't always get it right

Get comfortable with the idea of being wrong sometimes. No-one is infallible, and there will always be times when things don't work out quite how you expect. Putting too much pressure on yourself to get it exactly right all the time will just lead to you becoming scared of making any decision at all. That said, remember that very seldom is there such a thing as a 'wrong' decision. Each decision you make will have consequences, and it's a case of trying to anticipate those with the information you have available. Ultimately, you will need to make your judgement call, and your gut instinct is something that you should be able to rely on as you become more experienced in your field.

Finally, in terms of your career management, let me re-emphasise that there are very few decisions you could make that will have a permanent impact on your career. It's nearly always possible to revisit decisions, change direction or tweak what you are doing. Any career decision you make is only a decision for the next stage of your career – it's unlikely permanently to close other doors for you. So don't put off making a career decision that you are faced with – much better to take action and make progress than to dither endlessly and start to stagnate. Every decision you make is a learning experience. And remember the old adage that we are more likely to regret the things that we didn't do than the things that we did.

A decision isn't a decision until it's backed up by action

You can spend as much time as you like on making your big decisions, but nothing will change until you implement the choice you've made. I see this quite a lot with clients: they 'decide' that they're going to change job, they 'decide' what line of work they want to move into – but they don't do anything about it. That's not really a decision at all! Once you've made your decision, take action as soon as you can. You've given the issue plenty of thought, it's unlikely that dwelling on it further will improve your plan – so just get on with it.

REAL LIFE

Catherine came to see me three years ago to discuss her options for a career change. An office administrator, she was really drawn to the idea of primary school teaching. She did all the right things: researched the different training options, work-shadowed for a couple of weeks at her local primary school, and spoke with friends and contacts within the profession. Yet, although she'd 'decided' to re-train as a teacher, all this time later she still hasn't done anything about it. I think she's afraid of making the 'wrong' decision. But she's only going to know if it's the right decision if she actually gives it a go! In the meantime, she's simply wasting time.

IN A NUTSHELL

- Get comfortable with making straightforward decisions quickly: don't use them as an excuse to procrastinate.

- For bigger decisions, get as much information as you can. But don't ignore your gut instinct: a good decision will 'feel right'.

- Don't expect to get it right all the time. As the saying goes, people who never make mistakes never make anything!

If you'd like to learn more about decision-making, I recommend: Steps to Success, *Make Effective Decisions: How to weigh up the options and make the right choice,* A&C Black Publishers Ltd, 2007.

A short and straightforward book that sets out the best way to approach decisions, especially when under pressure.

23

Play to your strengths

We all have areas where we are naturally skilled. The more you can incorporate your natural strengths into your role, the more satisfying – and easy – your work will be. Equally, the less time you have to spend on tasks at which you are less accomplished, the less you will struggle at work. Focus on your strengths, therefore, and learn how to manage and compensate for your weaknesses.

Recognise your strengths

In Part 1 we looked at the importance of identifying your key skills and strengths. There's a difference between the two, in my opinion: your skills are the tasks that you are good at, but strengths go one step further. The areas where we tend to be really strong are where we not only are good at the task in hand, but where we actively enjoy it. So, for example, you might be good at writing, or presenting, or administration, but if you don't really get a 'buzz' from these things, then you're never going to be truly brilliant at them. Think of your strengths as the areas where your skills and your interests coincide: not only are you good at something, but you enjoy it, thrive on it and feel 'in the flow' when you're doing it. Your real strengths are the skills and traits that come most naturally to you. If you haven't already done so, this is a good time to take the strengths test recommended in Chapter 3.

Think also about your biggest achievements in your career so far. Which jobs or role have you most enjoyed? Look for the common themes that emerge: for example, perhaps you've really enjoyed both management roles and roles that required you to develop new business. The roles themselves may have been quite different, but the common theme could be that you are strong on relationship building. Being as aware as you can of the areas where you naturally excel – and we all have them – will help you to carve out the kind of role that suits you best.

Play to your strengths

Once you've come up with your list of strengths, think about ways in which you can tweak your role so that it reflects as many of them as possible. Try some of the following.

- **Talk to your boss.** Tell them what you most enjoy about your role, and the kinds of circumstances and activities where you feel that you perform best. It's in your manager's interest to help you maximise your performance, so don't be afraid to make suggestions for tasks that you'd love to concentrate more on, and those that other members of the team might be better placed to do. This isn't about dumping the less interesting bits of your job on to your colleagues – it's about showing your boss that you are thinking about the needs of the team as a whole, and how you can best play your part.

- **Expand your role.** You might find that the only way to incorporate more of what you like doing into your role is to take on extra responsibilities. Of course there's a limit to how much work one person can take on, but if you can identify opportunities to do more of what you love, then go for it. Your overall level of job satisfaction will go up, and if you're taking on tasks where you are naturally strong, you may find that you actually don't have to work much harder to achieve a lot more.

- **Volunteer.** If there really aren't any opportunities for you to formally expand your role, then think creatively! What other projects at work could you get involved in, or offer to help out with?

MAKING IT WORK IN PRACTICE

Playing to your strengths
A good rule of thumb is to ask yourself: 'Do I have an opportunity to make use of my key strengths every day?' If the answer is 'no', then use the approaches above to try to find ways of changing the emphasis of your role. If this isn't possible, then you really owe it to yourself to think about your long-term prospects in your current role – you may well be better off in a different job.

Manage your weaknesses

Just as we all have strengths, we also each have areas of 'weakness': tasks that we don't enjoy or do well, traits and behaviours that let us down from time to time. Conventional wisdom has dictated that we should concentrate on correcting our weaknesses. I expect that you've had work appraisals in the past where your boss has identified 'areas for development'. In other words, things that you need to learn to do better. Personally, I think that this is usually a fairly unhelpful approach. If you're not naturally good at something, it's going to take you a disproportionate amount of effort to get your skills to a high standard – and you'll still never be able to compete in performance terms with someone to whom that particular skill or attribute comes naturally. Far better, in my view, to expend your effort building on your own particular strengths, and minimising the amount of time that you have to spend on tasks at which you are less skilled. That doesn't mean that you should ignore your weaknesses and pretend they don't exist, but it does mean that you shouldn't spend disproportionate amounts of time trying to develop skills that don't come easily to you. So, what are the best ways to 'manage' your weaknesses?

- **Develop a coping mechanism**. For example, if you're nervous about speaking up in meetings, prepare what you're going to say in advance, or if you have a tendency to procrastinate or be disorganised, put systems in place to help you manage your time better. Dealing with your weaknesses in advance means they don't become as big an issue later on.

- **Recognise that 'good enough' is often good enough**. You don't have to be brilliant at everything. Sometimes, just being competent is good enough. Don't waste your time and energy trying to improve your performance in areas that don't really matter for your role.

- **Lean on other people**. It's not a sign of weakness to recognise that your colleagues are better at some things than you. If you're struggling, ask for their help. Remember that you're supposed to be working as a team, so help them out when you can and don't be too proud to ask for help when you need it.

The weaknesses you DO need to conquer

There are, however, some weaknesses that you can't afford to have if you are going to excel at work. Obviously, these will vary depending on your role and industry sector. If you're in advertising, for example, you're not going to get very far unless you can come up with creative ideas and write compelling copy. But there are some skills and strengths that are common to all jobs, and without which you'll really struggle to be successful. I would say that the most important of these are communication skills and thinking skills. If you can't put together logical arguments and plans of action, communicate them effectively to other people, and get them on board, you'll struggle to go very far in your career. We've looked at these skills in detail in earlier chapters, so if you feel that you're not as strong a thinker or communicator as you need to be, this is the time to re-read Chapters 19 and 20!

REAL LIFE

My client Sarah worked for a public relations company, where making business pitches to prospective clients was an important part of the role. Sarah's problem was that she hated presenting and speaking in public. She knew that if she couldn't improve her presentation and communication skills, she'd find it hard to progress further in the organisation. So she swallowed her pride and asked for extra training; went along to presentations by colleagues who were more fluent than she was to pick up tips; and made sure that, in advance of any pitch, she gave herself plenty of preparation time to ensure that she was as knowledgeable about her subject as possible. All of her effort paid off as she began to feel much more comfortable when presenting, and her increased confidence in turn helped to raise the quality of her presentations.

If you're a manager...

If you're in a management role, you need to be aware not just of your own strengths and weaknesses, but also of those of your team. Make the most of your team's skills and abilities. Let individual team members play to their strengths. Be flexible and creative: think in terms of the overall output that you need from your team, rather than just their individual job descriptions. Don't be afraid to 'mix and match': for example, if someone who has been hired to be the office manager shows a real skill for creative thinking, involve them in your planning meetings. If one of your sales consultants has a real flair for IT, give them the opportunity to help out with preparing presentations. Of course you need to make sure that individual team members are happy to take on extra or different responsibilities, and most of the time they will be: it's an opportunity for them to enrich their role and get more satisfaction from it.

If there are people on your team who are strong in areas where you are weaker, lean on them. Not only will it make your own job easier, but it will give your staff the opportunity to take on more responsibility, do work that they enjoy, and shine in their own right. They won't criticise you for your 'weakness'; they're more likely to respect you for recognising your limitations and giving other people the chance to show what they can do.

IN A NUTSHELL

- Your real strengths lie in the tasks you not only do well – but also enjoy.

- Play to your strengths as much and as often as you can, by tweaking your role, taking on new responsibilities, or even volunteering to help out in other areas.

- Learn to manage your weaknesses, but don't dwell on them. Focus and build on the positives of your performance.

If you'd like to learn more about playing to your strengths, I recommend:
Martin E P Seligman, *Authentic Happiness*, Nicholas Brealey Publishing, 2003.

Thought-provoking chapters on identifying your signature strengths and applying them at work.

24

Develop charisma

The way in which you approach your work and treat the people around you is fundamental to your career success. You are far more likely to become known, and remembered, for your attitude than for your skills and abilities – because it's your attitude that is always visible. Enthusiasm, kindness and a genuine concern for the needs of others are some of the attitudes that will help to propel your career forwards, because they are all aspects of one of the most important success factors – charisma.

The secret of charisma

What's the secret of charisma? It's one of those qualities that we recognise when we see it, but that can be hard to define. In my experience, charismatic people tend to be positive and enthusiastic; they believe in themselves; they display kindness and empathy; they have presence. And I think there's one further attribute that charismatic people display – they're great listeners. Here are my tips for the kind of charismatic behaviours which will help you succeed.

Enthusiasm is catching

A positive attitude is a great asset. Think of people you know who always see the negative side of things, and how draining they can be. In contrast, someone who is upbeat, who approaches tasks and problems in a constructive way, is someone that other people want to be around. People who tackle their work with enthusiasm are great people to work with.

I'm not talking here about the kind of people who are gushing, or declare that everything is 'wonderful' all the time, even when it clearly isn't. What we're talking about is 'intelligent enthusiasm': genuine enthusiasm for, and interest in, the task in hand. Think about what employers really look for when they are recruiting: someone who can do the job, of course, but also someone who wants the job, and someone who will fit into the organisation. The last two of these criteria can be the most important. Often, the person who gets the job is the one who demonstrates most clearly that they really want it. My friend Ally, who's a recruitment consultant, maintains that 'enthusiasm can take even talentless people a very long way'! That's because everybody wants to work with people who are positive, constructive and interested in what they do.

Kindness

Kindness usually costs nothing. But a small act of kindness can make a huge difference to someone else's working day. And it's not all about altruism either – kindness makes you feel good about yourself, and simply makes you a person that people want to have around. You'll find that you get back what you give out.

Kindness in the workplace has been around for a long time – think community volunteering and philanthropy for example. In today's business world, it's even more popular: companies are embracing corporate social responsibility (CSR) like never before. It's easy for the cynic in us to say that the reason for this is straightforward publicity and public relations, but for lots of companies, I believe it's about much more. It's a recognition that 'giving something back' benefits their business in all sorts of tangible and intangible ways.

Acts of kindness don't have to be big to be significant. Think about the little things that you can do at work to brighten other people's day. That could be something as basic as a cheery greeting, or making someone a cup of tea, or bringing some chocolate brownies into the office! Kindness oils the wheels of our relationships and just makes work a nicer place to be.

REAL LIFE

My former colleague Rachel is one of the kindest and most thoughtful people that I know – and everyone respects her enormously. She would always be the first person to offer to help if someone else was struggling with their workload, or the person who'd make everyone a cup of tea when we were flagging mid-afternoon. Just simple acts of thoughtfulness and kindness, but they had a disproportionate effect on the happiness of the whole office and made Rachel the person everyone wanted to work with.

Develop your presence

Are you the kind of person who lights up a room when you walk into it – or does no one notice that you're there? Charismatic people have presence. I think the term 'presence' embraces a number of things.

It's about how you carry and present yourself, how much gravitas you have, and how convincingly you communicate. So, to develop your presence – and your level of charisma – be aware of the following.

- **How you look.** Appearance is so important that we'll cover it in detail in Chapter 26, but for now, think about the people whom you would describe as charismatic. I bet they're not scruffy, untidy and badly-groomed. People with presence 'look the part'.

- **How you speak.** Your pitch and tone of voice speak volumes (no pun intended!) about your confidence and composure. People with presence don't gabble, or whisper, or 'um' and 'er'. Their speech is measured and rich and they're easy to listen to.

REAL LIFE

The most charismatic person I have ever met was Rudi Giuliani, the former Mayor of New York. I only spoke with him for a few minutes, but during that time he made me feel as if I was not just the most interesting person in the room, but the only person in the room. Closer to home, my friend Jennifer, an MD of a successful PR company, oozes charisma. She takes a passionate interest in everyone she meets, she listens and asks questions much more than she talks about herself, and every time I meet her I go away with a spring in my step. That's charisma. Work on developing your own brand of charisma, and watch your career progress upwards.

The power of positive language

How's your language? How often do you listen to how you really come across? All too often, our language can be negative or defensive, without our even realising it – even if we're not *feeling* negative. There

are the best part of a million words in the English language. How many
times do you choose to use a negative word instead of a positive one?
The classic example of this is how we respond when someone asks
'How are you?' Is your typical response 'fine' or 'not bad'? Doesn't
sound too upbeat, does it?

Unsurprisingly, our choice of language has a strong impact on how
people perceive us, and how receptive they are to our message. One of
the most negative words we can use is the dreaded 'but'. When people
hear this word, they know that an objection is coming. It doesn't
matter how positive what you have just said might have been, as soon
as someone hears 'but', all they will focus on is the negative statement
that follows.

TIP

*Stop using the word 'but'. If you have to make a critical comment,
preface it with something positive. Then simply start a new
sentence stating your criticism or concern. It will sound much
more balanced, and the person you're speaking to is more likely to
remember the positive things you have said too.*

The other phrase that most of us have a tendency to overuse is 'I'll
try'. Your boss asks if you can get your report to him by the end of the
week, and you say 'I'll try'. Your friend asks if you can come to their
party and you say 'I'll try'. Often, we respond in this way because
we're actually reluctant to make a commitment. Unfortunately, it
simply makes us look weak. Take responsibility and make a proper
commitment: 'Yes, I can do that' or 'Yes, I'll be there'. And if you
can't get the report done on time, or you don't want to go to the
party, just say so, and explain why. Equally, words like 'hopefully',
'probably' and 'fairly' have the effect of watering down our message
and making us look indecisive. Have the courage of your convictions
and resist the temptation to 'hedge your bets' with this kind of
qualifying statement. You'll come across as much more positive and
confident.

MAKING IT WORK IN PRACTICE

Positive language

For the next week, make a determined effort to eliminate negative words from your language. You'll find that, not only do you yourself feel more positive, other people will respond much more positively to you.

IN A NUTSHELL

- Work on your own brand of charisma. Nothing will help your career to progress further and faster than being someone that other people love to be around

- Your attitude is the most visible part of your contribution at work. It's how people will judge you and remember you.

- Enthusiasm is a great attribute. Build a reputation for yourself as the person who tackles tasks wholeheartedly and takes a constructive approach to solving problems.

- Become known for being an optimist, not a pessimist.

- Be kind. Treat your colleagues as well as your customers with thoughtfulness and respect. It costs nothing and makes work a nicer place to be.

If you'd like to learn more about developing charisma, I recommend: Amanda Vickers, Steve Bavister and Jackie Smith, *Personal Impact: What it takes to make a difference*, Pearson Education Ltd, 2009.

An extremely practical read, with strong sections on 'likeability' and how to make a good first impression.

25

Challenge yourself

Seeking out and embracing new challenges is the best way to keep yourself energised and motivated at work. Regularly reviewing your performance will help you to identify areas for improvement and new skills that you can develop. Being prepared to challenge your attitudes and beliefs can have a dramatic effect on your performance at work.

No room for complacency

'Time and tide wait for no man', as the saying goes. Well neither does the world of work. There's no option just to stand still: if you don't constantly challenge yourself to grow and develop professionally, you'll end up going backwards. There will always be new people coming into your organisation: people who are younger than you and who have more up-to-date skills. If you want to continue to shine at work, you can't afford to be complacent, however good you are at your job. And, in any case, if you don't find ways of bringing new challenges into your work, you'll simply end up bored and stale.

REAL LIFE

I once managed someone who'd been in his job for quite a few years and had become really complacent. Although Ewan was bright and capable, he'd allowed himself to get into a rut, stopped learning, and began simply to do the bare minimum to get by. The quality of his work fell to the stage where I eventually had to take disciplinary action. If Ewan had worked to find ways to stretch himself and keep his work fresh, this situation wouldn't have arisen.

Challenging yourself isn't about putting yourself under unnecessary and pointless pressure. It's about recognising that there will always be new things for you to learn, that all of us have scope to improve professionally, and that it's good to stretch yourself and keep yourself fresh in your job.

Choose your challenges carefully

It makes sense to take a 'strategic' approach to seeking out new challenges. In other words, looking for opportunities to stretch yourself in ways that will really add value to what you already do. So, for example, there's probably little point in pushing yourself to learn a new software package that you'll never use; on the other hand though, finding the time to take a creative writing course will help you improve your writing skills more generally. As I've stressed before, we can't all be brilliant at everything – and you don't have the time to become an expert on every area of your business. So think carefully about where to focus your efforts, and choose your challenges carefully. Don't waste time and effort building up expertise that no one needs or values!

Review your performance

Challenge yourself to be the best that you can be at your job. To do that, you need to be clear about what you already do really well, and where there is room for improvement. Get into the habit of regularly reviewing your own performance, and honestly assessing where you need to put in more effort.

MAKING IT WORK IN PRACTICE

Challenge yourself
Take time on a regular basis – once every three months, say – to sit down for half an hour and review your performance over that period. Ask yourself these questions:

- *what's gone well at work?*

- *what hasn't quite gone according to plan?*

- *what mistakes did I make, and what successes did I achieve?*

- *what will I do differently or better next time around?*

- *what opportunities did I shy away from?*

Be honest with yourself: this is for your eyes only. Being aware of what's going well and where you need to make improvements will help you to focus your efforts more effectively.

Don't just rely on your own appraisal of your performance! Ask for feedback. I hope you have a regular, formal appraisal with your boss or line manager but, if it's only an annual event, try to set up a conversation every couple of months or so, where you can actively seek out feedback on your performance. What opportunities are there for you to take on new challenges? What's changing in your office or your organisation, and what can you do to equip yourself to deal with new developments? What skills do you need to work on if you are hoping to move to the next rung on the ladder? Making clear that you are 'up for' new challenges will mark you out as someone who is committed to your job and your company.

Try new things

In Chapter 23 I stressed the importance of playing to your strengths – and I stand by that 100%. That said, it is good for us to get outside our comfort zone from time to time, to try new things and keep growing. Pushing yourself to have a go at something you haven't done before – whether that's giving a presentation, writing an article or organising an event – will help to keep you fresh and interested in your work. And you might discover new hidden talents!

Compete with yourself, not other people

Challenging yourself isn't about competing with other people, however. You don't have to strive to be the 'best' at everything. No one likes to work with someone who is overly-competitive, who always needs to 'win', or who tries to show others up. People want to work with colleagues who are supportive, and who care more about the collective results of the team than about their own successes. But you should strive to be the best that you can be. So challenge yourself constantly: to raise your standards, to learn new things, to become a better manager. Set yourself goals and targets. Compete with yourself.

Challenge your beliefs

Our attitudes and beliefs can let us down more often than our actions. We all know that some people view the glass as 'half-empty' and others see it as 'half-full': which are you? Do you tend to think in terms of 'problems' rather than 'challenges'? Do you regularly use words like 'catastrophe'? Do you find yourself thinking things like 'It'll never work'? Our beliefs are the single biggest factor affecting our behaviour. Recognising your belief patterns – and being prepared to challenge them – can have a huge impact on your performance at work.

The problem is that often our beliefs about ourselves are flawed: either they're based on other people's judgements ('My mother always told me I was lazy', 'My teacher told me I wasn't creative'), or they're based on generalisations we draw from one specific incident (you once gave a presentation that didn't go very well, so you think 'I am rubbish at public speaking'). Once a negative belief has taken root, we have a tendency to find further examples that reinforce that belief, and ignore evidence that might undermine it. So, in the public speaking example above, you reinforce your belief that you're no good at giving presentations by recalling only those instances where they haven't gone very well, and you filter out incidences where actually you performed absolutely competently. You end up with a distorted view of the situation and guess what: it becomes a self-fulfilling prophecy. Because you've convinced yourself a you're no good at speaking in public, that ends up being the case.

Combating negative thinking

How do you combat this negative thinking? Try to step back and look at the situation objectively. To continue with the public speaking example, you could make a list of all the occasions recently when you've had to speak in public. How would you grade your performance on each occasion? It's highly unlikely that you were truly dreadful every time! Can you ask a trusted colleague or customer for feedback? Even better, can you arrange for your next performance to be recorded, so that you can see for yourself what went well and what less well? Imagine that it's someone else speaking and not you: how would you rate your performance if you were a stranger? Bringing as much objectivity as you can to your judgement of yourself will help you to assess your performance more accurately.

Ultimately, it's down to you what you believe about yourself and the world around you, and in turn to determine your attitudes, actions and outcomes. Often we use our beliefs as an excuse for staying in our comfort zone. If you allow yourself to believe that you're not clever/creative/organised enough to set up your own business, for example, you've given yourself the excuse not to do anything about it. But if you allowed yourself to think that you *could* be capable of coming up with a good business idea, or you could have the self-discipline to make self-employment work for you, then you might actually have to do something about it and that would be scary!

I'm not advocating relentless optimism about every situation: an over-optimistic approach can lead people to take risks, misjudge situations and over-estimate their own ability. But most of us err on the side of not believing strongly enough in ourselves and of seeing the negative side of situations. We can afford to be more positive!

IN A NUTSHELL

- Don't allow yourself to get bored or complacent at work. Seek out new challenges and keep trying new things.

- Look for challenges that are relevant and will add value to what you do. Don't waste your energy on things that aren't worthwhile.

- Be aware of – and be prepared to challenge – negative thinking and attitudes.

If you'd like to learn more about challenging yourself, I recommend:

John Leach, *The Success Factor: Master the secret of a winning mindset,* Crimson Publishing, 2010.

A great book to dip in and out of, full of ideas for how to challenge yourself and your thinking to achieve success.

PART 3

MANAGING YOURSELF

In Part 2, we saw how managing your relationships correctly can really help you to shine at work. But you also need to manage yourself in the best way. That means maintaining high personal standards, being in control of your time and your workload, knowing where you need to focus your efforts – and doing it. It also means being able to handle stress, keep your sense of perspective, and above all, enjoy yourself at work. In this part of the book, we'll look in more detail at how to manage yourself and your work to help you get to the top.

26

Keep your standards high

To shine at work, you need to behave impeccably at all times. Know what your personal standards are, and stick to them. Ultimately, your standards outline how you treat other people – and will be reflected in your reputation.

Appearance matters

Appearance really, really matters. Why? Because, whether it's fair or not, we all make instant judgements about anyone we meet, based on what they look like. If they're smartly dressed, we're more likely to assume that they are professional, clever and successful. If they're scruffy and down-at-heel – we're less impressed.

Your appearance at work also says a lot about how well you fit in. Think about any time you've been for an interview: chances are you thought fairly carefully about what you would wear because you wanted to 'look the part'. It's the same on a day-to-day basis – what you wear reveals more than you might think about your attitude to work, and where you see yourself going in the organisation.

So, the first rule of thumb is: dress to fit in. If everyone in your department wears smart suits and ties, don't come to work in an open-necked shirt and jeans. If the female employees always wear skirts and high heels, don't wear trousers. Observe the dress code, even if it's unwritten (which it probably is). What's the point in drawing attention to yourself for all the wrong reasons?

If in doubt, dress like your boss, not your colleagues! This isn't about being flashy, or having ideas above your station, it's about acknowledging the fact that if you want people to see you as someone who is a rising star and going places, then you need to dress accordingly. Look at the people you admire in your organisation. How do they dress? What are the little touches that make them look like a senior employee?

When I worked in recruitment, I never ceased to be amazed by the number of people who would turn up for an interview – often for a fairly senior role – looking like they'd just rolled out of bed. Scruffy shoes, stains on their tie, daringly low-cut blouses: you name it, I've seen it all. If you don't look as if you are a senior operator, why would anyone think that you could be?

Set your standards

Image, of course, is not enough: not only do you need to look the part, you need to act the part. That's not just about doing your job well: it's also about the standards of behaviour that you adhere to.

We saw in Chapter 17 that every office has its own rules for behaviour, both written and un-written, which you need to be aware of and to conform with. But there are certain standards of approach and behaviour that should apply regardless of your office environment or culture. These are the behaviours that will help to mark you out as a true professional. Many of the attitudes and actions that I list below will (I hope) be no-brainers, and approaches that you already adopt. If not, then get ready to up your game

Be trustworthy

I hope this goes without saying, but it's worth taking a moment or two to think about what being 'trustworthy' actually means. Yes, it means being honest and not telling lies (see below), but I think it goes further than that. Being trustworthy is about being discreet. Literally, it means being 'worthy of trust'. So if someone shares a piece of confidential information with you, it goes no further. If someone asks you for advice in confidence, it's given in confidence. You can also argue that someone who is trustworthy does what they say they will do, when they say they will do it, meaning that reliability is part of being trustworthy.

The benefits of building a reputation for being trustworthy are obvious. People will confide in you, share information with you and rely on you. But it's a standard that you have to stick to 100% of the time. There's no such thing as being 'quite' trustworthy: you either are or you aren't.

Don't lie

Quite simply, lying is a mug's game: at some point you will get caught out. Whether it's a 'small' lie about why you are late in submitting your monthly report, or a much bigger lie about your qualifications or level of expertise when you're applying for a job, just don't do it. You should never decide that a lie about your work is small enough that it doesn't matter. Someone else might take a totally different view, and before you know it, you're facing disciplinary action. The easiest approach is therefore never to lie.

REAL LIFE

When I worked in recruitment, one of my colleagues once put a candidate forward for a job, which the candidate was subsequently offered. Unfortunately, when the employer asked for copies of the candidate's degree certificate, it emerged that he hadn't actually completed his degree, although he hadn't stated that on his CV. The job offer was promptly withdrawn, and the candidate's reputation was in tatters. It wasn't the fact that the candidate didn't have a degree that caused the problem, it was the fact that he had been dishonest about it. He paid a high price.

What about 'white' lies? Are they ever permissible? As I've made clear, I don't think it's ever permissible – or wise – to lie outright, but I do think that there are occasions when you can choose to be diplomatic, rather than blunt. So, for example, if a colleague asks what you thought of their presentation, and you actually thought it was pretty rubbish, it's probably better not to say exactly that! Equally, don't tell them that it was brilliant: they won't thank you for that if their boss subsequently slates them for a poor piece of work. So the rule is: spare people's feelings where you can, but don't say something that is wholly untrue.

Observe the common courtesies

How many times have you become irritated because a colleague asks you for something without so much as a 'please' or 'thank you'? Don't ever be guilty of the same behaviour. Courtesy costs nothing, it smoothes the wheels of your interaction with other people – and it's simply good manners. If you stopped a stranger in the street to ask for directions, you'd say 'please' and 'thank you' wouldn't you? Well, the people you work with are much more important to you than that stranger so you should extend them at least the same level of courtesy. If someone helps you out at work, make sure that you thank them immediately and explicitly. Praise, recognition and courtesy are the behaviours that make other people feel appreciated at work.

Never lose your temper

No matter how much someone at work has annoyed you, or let you down, never lose your cool. Losing your temper is a sign of weakness: it means you have lost control. That doesn't mean that you can't express your displeasure, though. If a member of your team has messed up on a piece of work, for example, or missed a deadline, of course you need to take them to task about it. But the best way to do that is calmly: let them know you are disappointed, but don't give them an excuse to get defensive or gain the moral high ground because you've shouted at them.

If you find yourself in a public situation where you are getting angry – perhaps colleagues are messing around in the office when you are on a really right deadline, for example – the best thing to do is walk away for a few minutes. Go outside, take some deep breaths, then get back to work and rise above it. Losing your cool just makes you look very un-cool.

Don't bring your personal problems to work

I don't mean that you should never talk about your home life. It's good for you and your team to know a bit about each other: how many kids you've got, what football team you support, where you're going for your holidays. This kind of office chit-chat makes people feel involved and closer to their colleagues. But, trust me, no one wants to hear the details of the messy divorce you're going through, or your child's problems at school, or the fact that you've had another row with your mother-in-law. They've got enough problems of their own.

If you do have a personal crisis going on, don't try to deal with it in the office. Leave it at home. If you genuinely need some time off to deal with a personal problem – a sick relative, a broken boiler, whatever – then speak privately to your boss and explain the situation calmly. Try not to get emotional – just state the facts and ask for the time out that you need. And don't be tempted to tell them the whole, sorry saga: keep it brief. It may seem like a huge problem for you, but your boss and colleagues will find it hard to share your degree of distress. Don't expect them to.

Don't bitch

As we saw in the chapter on managing office politics, it's all too easy for normal office banter to spill over into bitchiness and gossip. Don't go there. The golden rule is simple: don't say something behind anyone's back that you wouldn't say to their face. It's not just because there is a chance your comments will get reported back to them: it's because it's just not a nice or professional thing to do.

If other people are having a gossip, or a bitch, or a moan in the office, don't join in. You can't help hearing what they say, of course, but you don't need to engage with it. Be someone who only says positive things, gives compliments or doles out praise. Bitching and gossiping just makes you look petty, lazy and negative. If you can't say anything nice, don't say anything at all!

Be punctual

This might seem like a relatively small, even trivial, point but, trust me, it's important. There are few things more irritating to colleagues, clients or managers than someone who is always late for meetings and appointments. Not only does it make you look scatty and disorganised – a bad thing in itself, obviously – it also gives the impression that you think that your time is more important than other people's. If you routinely keep people waiting, the message that you're sending out is that you don't respect them.

If your time management isn't the best, there are some easy rules to follow.

- Always make sure that you give yourself plenty of time to get to appointments.

- Don't start looking for your paperwork five minutes before the meeting is due to start – dig it out at the beginning of your working day and have it to hand.

- Don't give anyone any reason to think that you're not on top of your working day – and your game.

If you follow these simple tips then your time keeping will improve and you'll make a much better impression.

MAKING IT WORK IN PRACTICE

Keep your standards high
The single best piece of advice in terms of keeping your standards high is simply this: treat other people in the way in which you yourself would like to be treated. It's an old golden rule – and for good reason.

IN A NUTSHELL

- Other people will judge you on how you behave, not just on the quality of your work.

- Be clear about your personal standards, and don't deviate from them. You need to be consistently professional.

- High standards of behaviour are all about treating other people with respect: being trustworthy, courteous and punctual are all attributes that others will notice and appreciate.

If you'd like to learn more about keeping your standards high, I recommend:
Richard Templar, *The Rules of Work*, Pearson Education Ltd, 2010.

Simple and straightforward advice on how to behave impeccably in the workplace.

27

Beat procrastination

We're all guilty of procrastination at times, usually because we don't want to do something or don't know how to do it. The good news is that there are simple, straightforward techniques to help you stop procrastinating. Being aware of your favourite 'displacement activities' – the things you do when you are putting off doing something else – can also help you to avoid frittering time away.

Why do you procrastinate?

Procrastination is something we all do. Show me someone who says they never procrastinate and you're either looking at the most efficient and successful person in the world – or a fibber! The irony is that there are no upsides to procrastination – it makes us feel guilty, we hate the feeling of incomplete work hanging over us, and we usually don't even really enjoy whatever displacement activity we engage in while we're putting off what needs to be done. Contrast these negative feelings with the positive sensation of achievement we have from getting things done, and it seems bizarre that we can so easily spend – or, rather, waste – so much time procrastinating.

So why do we do it? There are all sorts of theories about why we procrastinate but, in my view, it generally comes down to one of two reasons: we don't want to do something, or we don't know how to do something.

'I don't want to do this'

Very few of us have jobs where we love absolutely every element of what we do. Whether it's the admin, the report writing, or the financial side of things, there are likely to be parts of your job that don't particularly excite you. But you still have to do them. Below, I'll give you some tips on how to encourage yourself to get on with the tasks that you tend to put off. But first, let me say this: if you are spending more than a quarter of your time at work doing things that you don't enjoy, it might be time to sit back and have a good think about how well your job really suits you. Life is too short to spend doing things that don't make you happy.

If there are only some parts of your work that you don't like, think about whether you can outsource or delegate these. Yes, there are people out there who love the things you hate! Perhaps you have a team member who really enjoys administration, and who could help you with your invoicing. Or maybe you really don't enjoy writing the departmental monthly newsletter, but there's an intern in the office who would jump at the opportunity to develop their writing skills. Obviously, you don't want to gain a reputation as someone who tries to dump the less glamorous aspects of their work on to other people, but just sometimes you may find that what you regard as boring, someone else might actually enjoy: maybe you can offer to swap some basic tasks or responsibilities with them?

It's also important to be clear about what your priorities are. We'll look at this in more detail in the next chapter but, for now, think about the sorts of tasks that you normally find yourself procrastinating over, and decide how important they actually are. It may be that you are wasting time and energy putting off doing something that doesn't really need to be done at all!

How to motivate yourself

If you can't outsource or delegate a task, and it does really need to be done, then you'll just have to do it yourself. Here are some ways to prompt yourself to get on with those dreaded tasks.

- **Tell yourself you'll just do five minutes.** The chances are that, once you get started, you'll keep going. If not, at least you've done five minutes!

- **Do the worst thing first.** The benefit of this approach is that the task you're dreading isn't hanging over you all day, and getting that one thing ticked off your to-do list will give you lots of momentum to keep going with other things.

- **Develop a routine.** Schedule tasks in your diary and allocate specific amounts of time for completing them. This can help you to combat displacement activity: a routine makes it very clear what you have to do and by when.

- **Bribe yourself.** Tell yourself that once you've completed the task, you'll treat yourself: a cappuccino, a glass of wine, or allow yourself to log off early.

- **Make yourself accountable.** Tell a colleague what task you need to complete and by when, and get them to check up on you. The prospect of having to admit to someone else that you haven't done something is often enough to spur you into action.

'I don't know how to do this'

Another common reason for putting things off is because we're not really sure how to go about the task in the first place. Perhaps you've been given a big project that feels so daunting you just don't know where to start. Or maybe you aren't confident that you will do a good job, so by delaying getting started and giving yourself less time to complete it, you can always fall back on the excuse that you didn't have enough time to do the task really well.

If you're putting off starting a task because you don't really know *where* to start, try the following.

- **Ask for help.** Your manager would much rather spend 10 minutes of their time talking you through what needs to be done, than find out the day before the deadline that you haven't made any progress. In any case, it's your manager's responsibility to make sure that you know what you're supposed to being doing and how to do it, so if in doubt, don't be too proud to ask. Much better to feel a little foolish for having to ask for help, than to look completely incompetent when you don't deliver!

- **Break the project down into small chunks.** Ask yourself what the next immediate action you need to take is. Perhaps you need some more information, or to make a phone call, or to get all the relevant paperwork together. Identify the very first step you need to take – and do it. Again, this is about building up momentum: getting started is often the hardest thing of all.

- **Accept that you can't do everything perfectly**. It's much better to deliver a 'good enough' report by the deadline you've been given, than to miss the deadline because you've been putting off doing something that you think you can't do brilliantly.

REAL LIFE

When I set out to write my first book, I felt really daunted. How on earth was I going to produce 60,000 words? The answer? A word at a time! By breaking the task down so that I concentrated on one chapter at a time, and scheduling the writing of those chapters into my diary, I was able to make the project feel manageable. My target was to write two chapters a day. And once I'd written those two chapters, I rewarded myself with some 'me' time. That really helped me to keep on track.

Analyse your timewasters

When you're procrastinating over a particular task, I bet you don't spend the time doing other useful things. You're much more likely to indulge in what we call 'displacement activities': things that probably don't need to be done at all, but that give us an excuse for avoiding the job we're putting off.

Be aware of your most frequent timewasters and take action to tackle them. Here are some of the most common ways of frittering away time, and how to deal with them.

Email

How often do you check your emails? I bet it's probably every few minutes! If you get an audio alert or a visual pop-up every time a new email drops into your inbox, it's hard to resist the temptation to see who's contacting you. The trouble is that it's a huge distraction. Even if you don't respond to the email then and there, it distracts your mind from the task in hand. Discipline yourself to check your emails just three times a day – first thing in the morning, just before or after lunch, and about half-an-hour before you go home. Yes, it's difficult to do this, but I promise you it will have a huge impact on your efficiency and effectiveness. Very few emails require an instant response, so don't be a slave to that little 'pinging' noise or pop-up window. In fact, turn them off!

Internet

It's all too easy to start doing some research on the internet and, before you know it, half an hour has gone by. The internet is a fantastic tool, but you need to be the master of it, not a slave to it. Restrict the time you spend 'surfing'. Give yourself a deadline to find the information you need, and then stop. The chances are that what you need will come up on the first page or two of whatever internet search you do – don't waste time digging deeper.

Meetings

In my view, these can be the biggest timewaster of all. Do you really need to be there? Do you need to be there for the whole meeting? If you're in charge of the meeting, make sure you have an agenda and a time-limit. If it becomes clear at any point that you don't have the information you need to make necessary decisions, postpone the meeting. Don't let meetings turn into pointless talking shops. Wherever possible, have a phone call instead of a meeting.

MAKING IT WORK IN PRACTICE

Tackling procrastination

What's on your current 'to-do' list that you're procrastinating over? There may be more than one thing, but for now, pick one task that you've been putting off, and commit to tackling it by the end of the week. Think about why you've been procrastinating, and use the tips in this chapter to help you get motivated to take action on that task. You'll find that the sense of relief and achievement you feel when you've done it will spur you on to deal with other things you've been avoiding.

IN A NUTSHELL

- There are absolutely no upsides to procrastination. It wastes your time and makes you feel bad about yourself.

- If you putting something off because you don't want to do it (but you have to), find ways of bribing and rewarding yourself to get the job done.

- If you're putting something off because you don't know how to do it, ask for help.

- Break tasks down into manageable chunks to help you start tackling them.

- Be aware of your timewasters and cut them out. They're just easy distractions from the work you really should be doing.

If you'd like to learn more about beating procrastination, I recommend:
Duncan Bannatyne, *How To Be Smart With Your Time*, Orion Books, 2010.

A highly readable time-management guide from the star of *Dragons' Den*.

28

Focus your efforts

People who excel at work are the ones who know what their priorities are and focus on them ruthlessly. They are clear about the activities that really add value, and they manage their time effectively. They understand the difference between tasks that are really important and those that are merely urgent. They're very good at imposing – and sticking to – deadlines. These are the people who seem to – and usually do – achieve far more in a day than their colleagues.

Know what's important

How much of your time at work do you spend on things that don't really add any value? Not just the 'timewasters' that we discussed in the last chapter, but other tasks that might appear to be urgent or even important, but that don't actually contribute much to your overall work goals.

You've probably heard of the Pareto principle: the rule that says that 80% of your results come from 20% of your efforts. In business, this might mean that most of your revenue comes from a relatively small proportion of your customers, or that there are a few key elements of your job description that are the most important in terms of your performance at work. If you're going to be truly effective as well as efficient, you need to be crystal clear about what your priorities are on a quarterly, monthly, weekly and daily basis, and be ruthless in directing your time towards those priorities

Focus on your priorities

So, how do you start focusing on these key elements? The starting point for directing your efforts more productively is to get clear about what your priorities are. Dig out a copy of your job description, and highlight the tasks and responsibilities that are most important. Not the ones you enjoy most, but the ones that make up the output that is most important to your team and your boss. What are the tasks you do that really add value? What part of your role would your department not be able to function without? If you're not sure what the critical elements of your role are, talk to your boss so that you get a clear idea of what they consider the essential parts of your job to be. They are responsible for assessing your performance, and it doesn't matter how hardworking you are if your effort is being directed towards the wrong tasks and goals!

It's a good idea to take 10 minutes at the beginning of every week, and then five minutes at the start of each day, to note down your key tasks. Ask yourself 'What do I need to achieve this week/today?'. The clearer you can be about how you need to be spending your time, the more likely it is that you will get the important things done.

Urgent doesn't always mean important

Make sure that you don't focus on the 'urgent' at the expense of the 'important'. It's easy to spend all of your time on tasks that have short deadlines, for example, while you neglect the key report that you've been asked to submit by the end of the month. And then, surprise, surprise, it's nearly the end of the month, and you get into a complete panic because you've only got a couple of days to write your report! Being able to differentiate between the tasks that you really need to devote time to, and those that you can ignore without consequences, will help you to perform well without having to work all hours.

A good way to avoid the kind of scenario I've just described is to schedule your tasks, not just your appointments, in your diary. That way, you know that you have allocated a specific time to work on something, so you avoid the problem of a deadline creeping up on you un-noticed!

One further tip: beware of 'elephants' – big tasks that don't seem big at the moment because they're so far in the future. So, for example, if someone asks you to speak at a conference in six months' time, it's tempting to agree without too much thought because it's a long time away. But the trick is to ask yourself 'If this event was next week, would it be a good use of my time?'. If the answer is no, then it's not going to be a good use of your time in six months – so don't accept.

Allocate your time

It's one thing to decide what your priorities are, but nothing's going to change until you start to allocate your time in accordance with them. A good way of getting clear about how much time you are spending on things that are important, and how much time you 'fritter' away, is to undertake a time audit.

MAKING IT WORK IN PRACTICE

Focus on your priorities

For the next two weeks, keep a diary of how you actually spend your time. You don't need to record everything down to the last minute, or even hour-by-hour, but make a note of the main activities that you are spending your time on. How well does this picture reflect your real work priorities? How much time did you spend on activities that aren't even on your job description? How could you have spent your time better, and what changes can you make to ensure that you do?

It's easy to get into the habit of saying 'I don't have time for XXX', but the truth is that you have the same amount of time as everyone else – and you have all the time there is. It's how you use it that makes the difference.

Work expands to fill the time available

Parkinson's Law states that work expands to fill the time available for its completion. In other words, if you've got a whole day to write a report, it'll probably take you all day! But if someone were to come in to your office mid-morning, and say that they really needed the report by 2pm, not 5.30pm, the chances are you'd get it done on time. When you've got more time to do something, you simply tend to work more slowly, get easily distracted and so on. Most of us have a 9 to 5 mentality: we know we have to spend all day in the office, and we manage our workload accordingly. But what if you could go home as soon as you'd completed your key tasks for the day? I bet you'd be a lot more productive!

So, as well as focusing on what's important, be clear about the amount of time that you really need to spend on tasks. At what point do you stop adding value and start wasting time? This isn't about being 'slapdash' or lowering your standards, it's about improving your performance by recognising that spending longer on a task doesn't necessarily mean the end result will be any better. Set yourself challenging (but not impossible) deadlines for each piece of work you need to complete each day, and see how much more productive you become.

REAL LIFE

I once had a member of staff, Toby, who was very conscientious about every piece of work he did. He would slave over a report for hours, always submitting his work at the eleventh hour. Although the quality of his work was invariably excellent, he could have saved himself a lot of stress by realising that the extra hours he spent on each report or briefing didn't really add any extra value. By setting himself tighter deadlines, and a 'cut-off' point for each report, he could have avoided spending so much time on last-minute tweaks that usually weren't necessary. And then he could have gone home earlier!

Tips for focusing on your priorities

Here are some of the practical tips and tactics that I personally find most useful in helping to focus. This isn't rocket science, but they do make a real difference to the amount of work I get through.

- **Only handle any piece of paper once.** Actually, I'll qualify that – you might need to pick it up twice. When you first get the memo, report, or whatever, you need to decide whether you are going to deal with it straightaway or, if not, when you are going to deal with it. If you're not going to deal with it now, decide when you *are* going to process it, put it in your diary, and then put it away until you deal with it. Apparently, we handle any one piece of paperwork an average of seven times before we actually do anything with it. What a waste of time!

- **Learn to read faster**. Most of us have lots of paperwork to deal with and reading material to get through. Improving your reading rate can make a real difference to your efficiency: go on a course or read a book about speed-reading to help you pick up the key techniques. I promise you that it will be time well spent. And don't read stuff you don't need to – for example, often the first and last paragraphs of an article or report will tell you most of what you need to know.

- **Employ the 'two-minute' rule**. If a task will take less than two minutes, do it now. Otherwise, put it in your diary and come back to it later.

- **Batch your tasks**. Group similar kinds of tasks together – whether that's emails, phone calls, sending out invoices or writing letters. Your brain finds it easier to switch between different subjects than between different kinds of tasks. So clear all your phone calls in one go – it doesn't matter whether they're personal or professional, client catch-up calls or new business development. It's more efficient to batch your work according to the type of task involved.

In Chapter 30, we'll look in more detail at how to put great systems in place for managing your paperwork and in-tray – and therefore your time.

IN A NUTSHELL

- It doesn't matter how hard you work if you're not working on the right things! Be very clear about your work priorities.

- Take time at the beginning of each day and week to list the key things you need to achieve, and allocate the time for these tasks.

- Don't confuse urgent tasks with important tasks. Just because something needs to be done soon doesn't mean that you need to spend lots of time on it.

- Spend time on the tasks that are important, but remember that work expands to fill the time available. Don't spend longer than you need to on a task just because the deadline hasn't arrived.

If you'd like to learn more about focusing your efforts, I recommend: Jurgen Wolff, *Focus: The power of targeted thinking,* Pearson Education Ltd, 2008.

A practical guide to identifying and focusing on your goals and managing your time.

29

Manage your energy

Energetic people are good to be around. They come across as motivated, confident and successful. If you want to shine at work, you need to keep your energy levels high. Don't let your work environment, your lifestyle or other people's attitudes drain you of energy.

Energy is a state of mind

Of course energy is a physical thing – and in a moment we'll look at the simple, practical actions you can take to boost your energy levels, but, first and foremost, we need to acknowledge that energy is connected to your state of mind. Energy comes from a positive attitude, curiosity about the world, a genuine interest in and engagement with other people. It comes from doing work that you really enjoy and are excited about; from constantly looking for the positives, not the negatives, in any situation. Below I've outlined the best steps you can take to help you achieve a positive state of mind – and therefore boost your energy.

Don't moan: act!

One of the most energy-draining attitudes is complaining. So, the next time you find yourself moaning about something – don't just sit there, do something about it! Perhaps you're complaining because your boss has given you too much work to do. Instead of complaining about it talk to your boss: explain what you've got on your to-do list, and ask them what's the most important stuff for you to tackle. Maybe you're moaning about a client who is being particularly tricky. Phone them up, take them out for a cup of coffee or a drink, and try to get to know them – and their concerns – a little better. Don't waste your energy sitting around complaining about problems that, with a little bit of thought and effort, you can fix.

You are what you say

How often do you find yourself saying 'I'm so tired', or 'I'm really stressed' or 'I've got so much work to do'? All of these things might well be true but focusing on negative feelings like this just drains your energy even further. So, if you *are* feeling tired, stressed or overwhelmed, try not to verbalise it. Focus on getting on with whatever it is you need to do, not on how you are feeling about it. Working through your to-do list will give you a sense of momentum and achievement – and help you to feel much better.

Stay away from negative people

Think about the people that you love to spend time with. Why do you enjoy their company so much? Probably because they're positive, cheerful, good fun, and you go away from having seen them feeling better about yourself and about life in general. Negative people have exactly the opposite effect. Either you get drawn into their depressing view of the world, or you find yourself getting irritated because all they seem to talk about is complaints and problems.

Just as allowing yourself to wallow in self-pity and complaints reduces your energy levels even further, so being around other people who are negative will drain you. Whether they're work colleagues, friends or family, you need to find ways of diluting their toxic impact. Life is too short to allow yourself to be dragged down by other people's negativity.

Handling negative people

So how do you handle negative people? If you can, stay away from them – but this is often more easily said than done, especially if the person in question is your boss, or a family member. If you can't avoid them entirely, then try to 'dilute' their influence: don't meet your mother-in-law on a one-to-one basis, for example; instead, try to arrange family gatherings where you can ignore her for at least some of the time. (This is not a personal example, by the way – my mother-in-law is wonderful!).

Obviously it's trickier if the person you want to avoid is a work colleague – or, worse, your boss. But you can still minimise the time you spend with negative people, and compensate by making more time for colleagues and friends who give you a 'lift'. If all else fails, and you absolutely have to spend time with these people, just don't humour them. Refuse to get drawn into their moaning, and move the conversation on to more positive subjects.

It might sound 'selfish' to suggest that you should remove negative people from your life. Of course we all have problems that we want to talk over with other people, and none of us can be 100% positive all of the time, but there's a difference between a friend or colleague wanting to talk through a specific problem, and seek your advice and moral support, and someone whose default setting is negativity, moaning and complaining. You don't want to be associated with these types of people in other people's minds. And you can't afford to be dragged down with them.

Manage your environment

So far, we've seen that energy is largely about your mindset and attitude. But physical factors also impact on your energy levels. A key influence on your energy is your working environment. A cluttered, messy and disorganised office or workspace will negatively affect your output and efficiency. Contrary to what some people believe, an overloaded desk isn't a sign of how busy or important you are: it's a sign of someone who is disorganised, and who isn't working as effectively as they could. It's not just the fact that having loads of paperwork lying around means that it always takes you longer to find the report or information that you're looking for; physical clutter also drains your energy. So, what can you do to improve your working environment and, as a result, your energy?

- **De-clutter.** We'll look at how to de-clutter in more detail in the next chapter on putting good systems in place but, for now, make a commitment to yourself that you are going to have a good old clear-out. It's been estimated that we never get around to reading around 80% of the paperwork that comes across our desks, whether that's industry magazines, long reports or memos that we are copied into by other people. If you're not going to do something with it – get rid of it! Having lots of paperwork lying around simply distracts you from the work that you really should be doing. And don't try to fool yourself that having a tidy desk makes you look boring, 'un-creative' or just not busy enough. It doesn't: it helps you to stay in control.

- **Get rid of 'niggles'**. Things that don't work properly or need to be fixed are a constant energy drain. It might be something as simple as a drawer that sticks, but every time you try to open or close it, it will be a source of irritation to you. Make a 'snagging list' of all the little jobs that need doing in and around your workspace, and set time aside to deal with them. It will save you a lot of time and energy in the long run.

- **Make work a pleasant place to be**. This doesn't mean you have to have family photographs or bunches of flowers on your desk – although by all means do so if it cheers you up! But making sure that your desk is tidy, your keyboard and computer monitor are clean, your book shelves aren't over-loaded, are all simple ways of helping you to feel in control and more energised.

Managing your physical energy

We all know the basic rules of living healthily and managing our energy: eat well, drink lots of water, take some exercise, get out in the fresh air when you can, get enough sleep. We know that we feel better when we do these things, and sluggish when we don't. So be disciplined with yourself. Keep a bottle of water on your desk, bring in a healthy lunch from home, take 10 minutes at lunchtime to go for a quick walk in the park. Build these simple habits into your daily routine and watch your energy levels rise.

Another good trick to help you maximise your energy is to plan your working day to fit around your natural body rhythms as much as you can. Are you a 'morning' person or an 'evening' person? When do you feel most energetic, or creative, or focused? This is the time to tackle your biggest projects or most difficult jobs. Each of us has a natural energy rhythm, so it makes sense to harness that to your advantage.

REAL LIFE

I am really, really not a morning person. I hate getting up early and I need a couple of cups of strong coffee before I can face anything. I find that my most effective time of day is late afternoon and early evening. So, if I'm working on a writing project, for example, that's what I tend to do between 4pm and 8pm. I try to use mornings for the more mundane tasks that require a bit less thought and effort. That way I'm making the most of my natural energy levels and putting less pressure on myself.

IN A NUTSHELL

• Energy is largely a state of mind. Being positive, upbeat and enthusiastic about your work will keep your energy levels high. Conversely, moaning about problems instead of doing something about them simply drains you – and other people.

• Stay away from negative people, or do what you can to minimise their impact on your day. You can't afford to have them drain your energy, or to be associated with their negativity.

• Take simple, practical steps to manage your work environment and your physical energy.

If you'd like to learn more about managing your energy, I recommend: Bill Ford, *High Energy Habits*, Simon & Schuster Ltd, 2002.

An extremely practical (and often very funny) guide to raising your energy by managing your work and home environment.

30

Put great systems in place

If you want to shine at work, you need to be organised and efficient. Being in control of your work is about knowing what you have to do and when you have to do it. And that in turn depends on having great systems in place to support you.

Master your workload

How often do you feel that you are drowning in work? However much effort you put in, your in-tray never seems to get any less full, and your list of tasks just keeps growing. You can't even remember some of what you're supposed to be doing! When we allow ourselves to get overwhelmed by emails and paperwork, we are out of control. The chances are we are going to miss deadlines, forget about an important piece of work, or fail to turn up at a crucial meeting. None of which helps us to shine.

If this sounds familiar, don't despair. There are straightforward and simple approaches that you can adopt to help you tame the monster that is your to-do list. The three key secrets to getting back in control of your work, and therefore your work–life balance, are to:

1. get organised

2. prioritise

3. get on with it.

Not exactly rocket science, is it? And that's the good news: anyone can get on top of their workload, just by following some basic steps.

Get organised

The number one secret to being in control of your work is to get organised in the first place. That might seem blindingly obvious, but we can waste a huge amount of time simply because we're not clear about what we have to do and by when. That's when deadlines creep up on us, and what could have been a straightforward task turns into a panic and crisis. What's more, trying to remember everything we have to do is in itself a major source of stress. How many times have you woken up in the middle of the night thinking 'I must remember such-and-such'? Or how often do you get distracted from the task you're working on because your mind is trying to remind you of other things you need to do? We waste a huge amount of time and energy trying to remember all the things we have to do! That's why most people's action or to-do lists are actually ineffective: because they're not comprehensive. Most of us write a 'selective' action list – we jot down some of the tasks we need to complete, but we've still got a load of 'stuff' floating around in our heads. So, the starting point for getting really, really organised is to compile a *complete* to-do list.

Making your complete to-do list

I'll be honest, this is quite a big project! It might take you as much as a whole day but I promise you that it will revolutionise the way you work. I do recommend that, however much you love your technology, you should carry out this job on a pen-and-paper basis: it really does make it more manageable. Arm yourself with a big pad of paper, and you're ready to go!

First of all, gather together all your piles of pending paperwork – reports, bills, memos you need to respond to, whatever. Once you've got them all in one place, go through the pile, and write the action that you need to take for each item on a single sheet of your paper pad, ie one page for each individual task. Then do the same for your email inbox. Finally, go around your whole office and note down any other tasks that need to be done that you haven't already captured – ordering new stationery, for example, or fixing the broken printer. This process will take a bit of time but, once you've done it, you will have a pile of paper that fully represents all your work tasks.

Now you need to organise those bits of paper! Basically, there are four actions that you can take with any one of those pieces of paper:

1. dump it

2. delegate it

3. do it

4. defer/diarise it.

Dump it

Most of us are overwhelmed with paperwork. Newsletters, circulars, financial reports, trade publications, you name it, our in-trays are overflowing. And yet we will never read around 80% of the paperwork that comes our way. Instead, we tend to stack it up, waiting for the day when we 'have time' to read it. Most of the time that day never comes or, if it does, the material is probably out of date anyway. So what's the answer? Simple: be ruthless! Give yourself a fresh start by getting rid of everything you don't need. If you know deep down that you're unlikely to read it – bin it. If it's something that you might want to refer to in the future, but you can quite easily access it elsewhere, online for example, then bin it. If it's a piece of information that you know you will definitely refer to in the future but don't need right now, then put it in your filing system – in such a way that you will be able to access it easily when you need to. If in doubt, err on the side of recklessness: there are very few pieces of information that you won't be able to retrieve from somewhere else if you really need them at some point in the future.

Being disciplined about de-cluttering your workspace in this way will reap rewards. You'll immediately start to feel more in control: you'll spend far less time wading through the stuff you don't need to find the stuff you do, and you're much less likely constantly to be distracted by all the information that's sitting there waiting for you, whether you really need it or not.

MAKING IT WORK IN PRACTICE

Getting organised
For the information you do need to retain, take the time to devise a good filing system – and keep it up to date as you go. You want to be able to access information that you need quickly and easily. Make sure that the files you use most often are the ones that are the easiest to retrieve.

Delegate it

Now you've got rid of all the extraneous stuff, you're ready to tackle your pile of actions. Go through your sheets of paper and decide which are the jobs that you can, or should, delegate. Who is better placed than you to carry out that task? It's easy to fall into the trap of thinking that by being a control freak, we are actually in control: we're not. Remember the Pareto principle: you need to spend your time on the activities that are most valuable to you and your organisation and that means giving work to the person best suited to do it.

Of course, if you don't have a team to whom you can delegate anything, or you are self-employed, then it's harder to offload work. The trick here is to be imaginative: who could help you complete this task or solve this problem? Sometimes a quick phone call to someone with more expertise than you can help you find a more efficient way of dealing with something. If you're self-employed, do consider the business case for outsourcing particular tasks. Think about how long it would take you to complete the job yourself, and what that would 'cost' you in terms of your time. If your time would be better spent elsewhere, find someone you can pay to do the job – who'll probably be able to do it more quickly and efficiently than you anyway.

Do it

As you work through your list of tasks and projects, whenever you come across an action that will take less than two minutes – do it now. This is a good way of clearing lots of little tasks from your action list, leaving the way clear for you to focus on the bigger projects. It's also a good way of 'catching up': once you've finished this exercise, whether it takes you a day or a whole weekend, you'll be back up to speed. If you maintain the two-minute rule, it means that you'll respond to emails more quickly, and deal with small tasks promptly, which in turn means that you'll be – and be seen as – more efficient. It means that you'll be in a position to be able to do *today's* work, not last week's. And that's a good feeling.

Defer/diarise it

Working through your list, when you come across a task that is going to take more than two minutes to complete, decide when you are going to do it. This is key: don't just transfer it into a 'pending' pile. Decide how long the job is likely to take, and put it in your diary. This approach has a number of benefits. Firstly, it will force you to think properly about how long a task is going to take, so that you can schedule it appropriately in your diary. It takes a bit of practice to forecast the length of jobs accurately – and of course there will always be occasions when factors outside your control affect your timings, but it's a good discipline to get into. Remember Parkinson's Law from Chapter 29? We waste a lot of time simply letting work 'drift' because we haven't been disciplined enough about the timescale.

Secondly, scheduling tasks in your diary will stop you from over-committing yourself on meetings. Often, meetings are the only things we actually put in our diary. The problem with that is that it's all too easy to forget to factor in preparation time, follow-up time, and the time we need for the other projects we're working on. Give the average manager (or their PA) a clear diary and chances are they'll fill it up with meetings, leaving no thinking or real action time. By scheduling your tasks in your diary, as if they were meetings, you'll help to ensure that you actually get the time to work on those tasks.

REAL LIFE

The tip that I have found most effective in helping me to manage my workload is to make sure that I schedule tasks, as well as appointments, in my diary. Otherwise, it's too easy to fill up my diary with client meetings, and then find that I don't have enough time to prepare for each appointment. By specifically scheduling in slots of 'preparation' time, it's much easier for me to control my workload, because I'm not tempted to overbook or over-commit myself.

Weekly reviews

Once you've carried out the one-off exercise of logging all your outstanding tasks, you just need to keep on top of it! A weekly review is normally sufficient for this, though sometimes you'll probably need to juggle things a little bit day-by-day. By reviewing your current and pending workload on a regular basis, and keeping your task list totally up to date, you'll feel much more in control, and find it much easier to deal with emergencies when they do occur, without losing sight of the bigger picture and your real work (and non-work) priorities.

IN A NUTSHELL

- You can't shine if you're not organised and in control of your workload. It's a basic rule.

- Set aside time to organise your workload and put good systems in place. Your initial time investment will be paid back many times over by your improved efficiency.

- Update your task list regularly, so that you never again get sucked into a backlog.

If you'd like to learn more about managing your systems, I recommend: David Allen, *Getting Things Done: How to achieve stress-free productivity*, Piatkus Books, 2002.

A comprehensive guide to helping you get in control of your workload once and for all.

31

Learn to say 'no'

People who excel at work recognise the power of saying 'no'. They know their priorities and won't let other people divert them from those priorities. Being able to say 'no' graciously is one of the skills that will help you to stay focused on your true goals.

The power of 'no'

At first sight, this strategy might seem at odds with what I've said elsewhere in the book about effort, volunteering and 'going the extra mile'. Surely saying no to someone's request for help will simply mark you out as someone who is unwilling, not prepared to collaborate and unmotivated – and this doesn't sound great for your career progression. But this is not necessarily the case: the secret is to know *when* and *how* to say no.

If you want to have a good work–life balance, the word 'no' simply has to become part of your vocabulary. If you don't tell your boss that you're already working at capacity, they'll keep piling things on to your workload. If you say 'yes' to every request for your time from colleagues, friends and family, you'll end up with no time to yourself at all. If you take on new work indiscriminately, you'll end up getting dragged further and further away from the outputs that you really want to achieve – and it's these outputs which your performance will be measured against. What's more, if you take on too much, you'll end up doing at least some of it badly – which is often worse than not doing it at all. It's much better to be honest about your workload and priorities at the outset.

Saying 'no' to yourself

Often the first person you have to say 'no' to is yourself!

A good approach is to get better at distinguishing between things you have to do, things you want to do, and things that you feel you 'should' do. The 'should' tasks can take up a disproportionate amount of your time. For example, you *have* to do your tax return or submit your end-of-month departmental report. You *want* to go to the cinema or attend a networking event. You feel that you *should* call your mother, or catch up with an old client, but these tasks should all have different priorities regardless of your feelings. Get into the habit of reviewing your to-do list, and identify whether the items on the list are 'must-do's', 'would-like-to-do's', or 'feel-that-I-ought-to-do's'. If you don't have to do something, and don't want to do it, then think about striking it off your list.

MAKING IT WORK IN PRACTICE

Eliminating 'should' do

*For the next week, eliminate the words 'should' or 'ought to' from your vocabulary. Every time you find yourself thinking 'I ought to do XXX', stop and give it some more thought. Do you **need** to do this task? Do you **want** to do it? If the answer to both questions is 'no' then you should seriously consider why this task is on your to-do list at all.*

When to say 'no' to other people

So, how do you decide when saying 'no' is going to be damaging to your career, and when it's the most sensible option? Here are some rules of thumb.

- **Make 'yes' your default option**. Most of the time, when you are asked to help out with a project, or take on a new responsibility, the clever thing to say is 'yes', enthusiastically and straightaway. But sometimes it's ok to say 'no'. Look at is this way: if you never say no, people won't attach much value to the fact that you've agreed to their request. You also run the risk of looking weak and unassertive – not to mention completely overloading yourself.

- **Make sure you know what's in it for you**. Sometimes you'll be asked to do something that doesn't have any obvious payback for you. Think carefully about these kinds of requests. You've only got a certain amount of time to work with, and if you spend too much of it on tasks that don't take your own career forward, you're not doing yourself any favours. That said, think about the long-term benefits of agreeing to something, not just the immediate payback. It might be that by helping a colleague out, you'll be able to call in the favour one day. Or by taking on a new area of responsibility, you're enhancing your CV for when you're ready to move jobs. So think laterally about how saying 'yes' might be helpful to you as well as to the other person. Just don't let yourself become a doormat.

- **Establish what you'll have to drop**. If you've been asked to do something that will only take a few minutes – proofread a colleague's report, for example – then it's unlikely to have significant implications for your own output. But if it's a bigger project, the chances are that something else will have to give. Ask yourself what that would be – and if the trade-off is worth it.

- **Bear in mind who you are going to disappoint**. It may sound a bit calculating, but it's important to take account of who it is that you will be disappointing or letting down if you say 'no'. If the Chief Executive asks for your help with something, a refusal isn't going to do your career prospects much good!

Also remember that it's much better to say 'no' at the outset than to agree to help out or undertake a piece of work, and then find yourself reneging on your promise or failing to meet the deadline. People will be much more irritated if you agree to their request but then fail to deliver or follow through.

REAL LIFE

Early on in my career as a coach, I fell into the trap of saying 'yes' to everything – I guess I thought it was what a coach 'should' do. So whether it was an invitation to speak at a conference, a request to do some 'pro bono' work, or an approach from someone interested in coaching who wanted to pick my brains, I'd always agree. The trouble was, I soon found that my diary was filling up with work that wasn't earning me any money! I had to become more discerning and disciplined about which requests I agreed to. Don't get me wrong: I'm very happy to help other people out – when I have the time. But I had to learn that the needs of my business and fee-paying clients had to come first – otherwise I wouldn't have a business!

How to say 'no'

So, when you need to, how can you say 'no' tactfully? Try the following techniques:

- **Hear the other person out**. Let them explain their request without interrupting, so that, even if you do refuse it, they feel that you've made that decision based on all the facts.

- **Explain the reason for your refusal**. Be honest: if your diary is already committed on the day they want you to make a presentation, say so. If you have more urgent tasks to complete, explain this. People will appreciate you being straightforward with them. And it's much better to refuse on the spot than to say 'I'll think about it', knowing that you really don't want to do the task and you'll end up going back to them a day or a week later and saying 'no' after all.

- **Offer to help in a smaller way**. Do consider whether, even if you can't accede to the other person's request in full, you might be able to help in some smaller way. For example, you don't have time to read the draft of their full report, but you'd be happy to offer comments on their key findings. Or you don't want to commit to the workshop they've asked you to run, but you'll recommend some other possible speakers. Actions like this allow you to be considerate of and helpful to others, without completely overloading yourself.

Saying 'no' to your boss

Of course, there's one person that it's very hard indeed to say no to – your boss. In Chapter 13, we looked at your responsibility to make your boss's life easier, not harder. How can you square that with saying 'no'? By remembering that it's in no one's interests for you to be so overworked that the quality of your work suffers. If your boss is piling more and more work on to you – and they generally will, until you squeal! – it's up to you to make sure that they know that you're not in a position to take on anything more. Force them to make a decision about which tasks are their priority – that's why they're the boss, after all. As with other people, though, saying 'no' to your boss is something that you should only do sparingly. If you normally say 'yes' when they ask you to take a task on, they should come to realise that on the occasions when you do say 'no' it's because you really, really can't take on anything more at the moment.

IN A NUTSHELL

- You can't do everything, so sometimes you will have to say 'no'. The trick is to be able to do it diplomatically.

- Being clear about your priorities will make it easier to make instant decisions about how to respond to other people's requests.

- Focus your efforts on the things you have to do and the things you want to do. Eliminate the things that you merely think you 'should' do.

If you'd like to learn more about how to say 'no', I recommend:
Leo Babauta, *The Power of Less: The 6 productivity principles that will change your life*, Hay House UK Ltd, 2009.

A clear and concise guide to achieving more by doing less, including through setting limits on your commitments.

32

Beat stress

It's easy to be positive, calm and in control when things are going well, but how you handle problems, and the stress that accompanies them, is the true measure of your professionalism. It's an attribute that will really set you apart from the crowd, and make people want to have you in their team or their organisation.

The cost of stress

The cost of work-related stress is well-documented. Research carried out by the National Institute for Clinical Excellence (NICE) in 2009 suggested that as many as 13 million work days are lost to stress-related illness every year, at a cost of some £30bn. Perhaps it's not surprising that stress at work is a growing problem: in a difficult economic climate, companies and organisations have had to make cutbacks, so that many workers have found themselves with bigger workloads, not to mention the threat of redundancy that has loomed over many people's heads. But, while there may be understandable reasons as to why many of us are feeling more stressed at work, the good news is that there is plenty that we can do to beat stress. You are more in control than you think!

Stress can be positive

We all expect to have a certain amount of pressure or stress at work. In fact, there are times when a bit of stress can be a good thing! Think about the last time you went for an interview, or gave a presentation. You probably felt nervous and anxious beforehand. But while the negative aspects of stress aren't pleasant – racing heart, dry mouth, sweaty palms – the adrenaline that kicks in when you're feeling under a bit of pressure can actually help you to perform better. Your attention is more focused, you think more clearly and your concentration goes into super-drive. Remember the 'rush' you felt when the interview or presentation was over (assuming it went well!). A certain amount of stress, from time to time, can be a driver that helps us to perform at our best.

Frequently feeling stressed is a different matter, however. We all have differing abilities to cope with stress, and we each respond to it in different ways. What's more, we all have our own individual stress 'triggers', and they're different for everyone. Some people seem to cope brilliantly when they're overloaded with work, but will fall apart if a client or colleague criticises them. Other people handle difficult relationships with ease, but get really stressed if they think they're going to miss a deadline. So the starting points for beating stress are to recognise the signs, and to be aware of what your personal stress triggers are.

What stresses you?

We don't get stressed for no reason: there's always an underlying cause. Being aware of your stress triggers can make it easier for you to avoid, or at least cope with, stressful situations, because you can see them coming. Typical stress triggers include:

- **having too much work to do:** you just don't see how you can possibly get everything on your 'to-do' list finished by the deadlines

- **being disorganised:** you can't find the report you need, and you're conscious that you're wasting time trying to find it

- **procrastination:** you've been putting off a task, the deadline is looming and you're starting to panic!

- **being a perfectionist:** you want to do everything to the highest standard, and beat yourself up if you make a small mistake

- **other people:** your colleagues are winding you up because their office banter is distracting you from the urgent task you need to complete.

Although we all experience difficult times at work, very often our stress is self-imposed. In the examples above, for instance, most of the stress triggers are down to your own behaviour: not being organised, putting work off, having unrealistically high standards. By recognising that, in many instances, you have the power to avoid these causes of stress, it becomes easier to take control.

Obvious as it may sound, the secret is not to focus on tackling your feelings of stress, but to deal with the issue that's causing them in the first place! So, if you're feeling disorganised and out of control, take the time to have a tidy-up and update your 'to-do' list. If you habitually procrastinate, start using the tips and techniques in Chapter 27 to help you manage your time better. If you always put yourself under pressure to do everything 'perfectly', remind yourself of your top priorities and focus on those. Don't let yourself become a victim of avoidable stress.

MAKING IT WORK IN PRACTICE

Avoiding stress
Think about the last time you were really stressed at work. Be honest with yourself: how much of your stress was self-inflicted or could have been avoided? What actions can you take to prevent the same problem arising again?

One further point that you need to be aware of is that you shouldn't allow yourself to fall into the trap of seeing stress as some kind of status symbol. We all know people at work who're constantly moaning about how busy they are, how much responsibility they have, and how stressed they're feeling. They seem to think that being 'stressed' makes them look important. It doesn't: it just makes them look as if they're not on top of their job!

Know what you can and can't control

While much of the stress we experience at work can be self-imposed, there will of course be times when other people, or simply circumstances, make our stress levels soar. Perhaps your boss keeps loading more and more work on top of you, or a client has criticised the report you prepared for them. Maybe your colleagues are winding you up. Or it might be something as simple as your train being late. These kinds of situations are stressful largely because we feel that we are not in control.

But, while you can't control your boss, your client, or your colleagues, (or even your train!), you can control how you respond. So, for example, if your boss has given you too much work to do, you can choose to say nothing and try to cope with all the work, or you can explain to them that you don't have the capacity to take on any more (see the last chapter for how to say 'no' to your boss!). If your client has criticised you, you can choose to sulk, or argue with them, or to acknowledge their criticism and work with them to make sure you deliver what they want next time around. If your colleagues are irritating you, you can choose to rise to the bait, or ignore them. Even if your train is late, you can choose to get irritated and impatient, or take the time to catch up on some reading. However little control you may feel that you have over the specific situation, you always have control over how you react to it. Recognising this will help you to feel much less powerless – and less stressed. So, if you start to recognise the signs of stress, the first thing is to acknowledge that your stress 'trigger' has been activated, and to step back for a moment to try to view the situation as objectively as possible. Just taking a few deep breaths or removing yourself from the situation for a couple of minutes can be enough to help you feel more in control.

If you're suffering from constant and prolonged stress, which is affecting your health, then that's another matter (see below), but assuming that stressful times at work are occasional and not permanent, you need to be able to handle these calmly and graciously. If you can build yourself a reputation as someone who never 'loses it', who doesn't panic and who stays in control of their emotions, you will be doing yourself – and your career prospects – an enormous favour.

Long-term stress

So much for how to handle one-off or occasional stressful situations, what do you do if your work is constantly stressful, to the point where you really feel that you can't cope any more? The first thing to do is to decide whether this is a temporary problem (for example, you're having to cover for a colleague who is off on extended sick leave) or a permanent one (for example, the nature of your job is that clients call you all hours of the day and night, and at weekends). If it's a temporary situation, you might decide that you can put up with it, or you may be able to talk to your manager, or HR, or someone else in the organisation who might be able to help you deal with the problem. If, however, it's a situation that is inherent to the kind of work you do – you are simply expected to take calls from clients at all hours, for instance then you need to decide if it's really worth it. If your work is causing you long-term stress, then frankly, it probably isn't worth it. So my advice is simple: walk away. Life is too short to spend it in a job that you're not coping well with – and how can you possibly excel in that kind of situation?

REAL LIFE

I worked with a client recently who came to me because she wanted to look at new career options. A corporate lawyer by profession, Lucy had just been signed off work with stress. Small wonder: she was literally working 18 to 20 hours a day, as well as weekends. We considered a whole range of other work options for her, and she ultimately decided to take on a part-time role in a smaller law firm, while retraining as an acupuncturist. She's much happier and less stressed and, although she's earning less money, the quality of her lifestyle is much higher.

IN A NUTSHELL

- How you deal with problems and stress is one of the key measures of your professionalism. Build a reputation for being the person who is calm in a crisis: it's a core attribute of successful leaders.

- Recognise that most stress is self-imposed: we are our own worst enemies!

- Even when you can't control a situation, you can control your response to it. Recognising that you have choices helps to reduce your sense of powerlessness – and stress.

- If you find yourself in a job that is permanently and relentlessly stressful, think seriously about walking away. No job is worth sacrificing your health for.

If you'd like to learn more about managing stress, I recommend:
Gillian Butler and Tony Hope, *Manage your Mind: The mental fitness guide*, Oxford University Press, 1995.

Down-to-earth advice on coping with stress and anxiety.

33

Keep your perspective

Successful people have a well-developed sense of perspective. They know where to focus their efforts, and when to give up or let go. They know what really matters and what doesn't. And they've mastered their 'work–life balance': they know how to do a great job but still go home on time.

Keeping work in perspective

In the last chapter, we looked at some of the most common 'triggers' for stress at work, and how to deal with them. One point that I didn't cover – because, in my view, it merits a chapter to itself – is the importance of keeping problems and challenges at work in perspective. It's all too easy to get stressed by a project that isn't running to deadline, or a mistake that you made, or a presentation that didn't go as well as you had hoped. But blowing things out of proportion doesn't help anyone. No one wants to be around the kind of person who turns every difficulty into a drama, or every minor error into a complete catastrophe. In contrast, the kind of people we do like to have around us are the ones who don't overreact, who keep calm, and who focus their energy on solving the problem or correcting the error. That's the approach you need to master if you want to excel at work.

Everyone makes mistakes; unexpected interruptions waylay even the most organised person; and no one gets it right all the time. Recognising that you are human, and that it's forgivable if everything isn't always perfect, not only helps you to manage your stress levels, but also keeps you focused on what's really important about what you do. Of course, that's more easily said than done! We all have a tendency to dwell on problems or mistakes, and often forget that most of the time we are doing a good job and things are going well. So, how do you keep problems at work in perspective? Here are some tried and tested approaches.

- **The week/month/year rule**. How much will the problem or mistake matter in a week, a month, a year? We looked at this approach in Chapter 22 on the context of making decisions, but it's a useful approach for keeping your perspective, too. If there aren't going to be any significant repercussions in the short-, medium- or long-term, then it's really not worth worrying about too much. On the other hand, if failing to address the issue *will* have ongoing consequences, either for you or your organisation, then it's clearly something that demands to be treated as a priority.

- **The 'water under the bridge' rule**. If you've made a mistake, apologise to whomever you need to apologise to, and do what you can to put things right, then move on. Take the opportunity to learn from the experience, but don't keep beating yourself up about it. You can't change what's happened, so don't waste time and energy fretting about it.

- **The 'worst-case scenario' rule**. Again, this approach is as useful for keeping issues in perspective as it is for decision-making. If you're faced with a problem that you're not sure how to solve, ask yourself 'What's the worst that could happen if I do XXX?' Chances are no one's going to die, or lose their job, and your company or organisation isn't going to fall apart. If any of these consequences *might* happen, then it's definitely time to ask for other people's input before you go ahead with your plan of action!

Ultimately, learning to keep things in perspective will make you a better employee. You'll spend less time worrying, and more time actually doing something constructive. I'm not suggesting in any way that your attitude to your work should be cavalier or blasé, I'm simply saying that most problems aren't as big as we let ourselves believe.

Work–life balance: the bigger picture

Keeping things in perspective isn't just about how you deal with your day-to-day work. It's also about how your work fits into your life as a whole. For most of us, one of the biggest challenges that we face is trying to juggle the demands of work with all of our responsibilities outside of work – our family, our partner, our friends, and of course ourselves. Full-time work takes up a big chunk of your week – 40 hours at least, and often more – and that's not including the time you might spend commuting to the office, thinking about work when you're not there, and so on.

The phrase 'work–life balance' is one that you hear a lot these days. In many ways that's a good thing; it shows that more of us, and more employers, are recognising that you don't have to sell your soul to the corporate devil to be successful, and that people actually work better when their work is not all-consuming. Perhaps the most important thing to remember is that there's no single, perfect definition of what constitutes a good work–life balance. It depends on what your personal priorities are, and it also depends to some extent on the stage you are at in your career. If you are in your twenties and thirties, trying to climb the corporate ladder and build a reputation for yourself, there will be times when work just has to come first, when you're working long hours and giving it everything you've got. And as long as that's part of your strategy to get to where you want to be, that's fine. But the bottom line is: don't work hard without knowing why. Put your work in the context of the 'bigger picture' of your life as a whole.

MAKING IT WORK IN PRACTICE

Achieving a work–life balance

However busy you are, and whatever crazy hours you work, make a promise to yourself that you will leave the office on time at least one day a week. Plan something specific to do – go to the cinema, or arrange to meet a friend for dinner. What's the point in working really hard to earn money to enjoy yourself if you never enjoy yourself?

Your work is not your life

I really want to stress this point: **your work is not your life**. It might seem like an odd statement in a book on career development; after all, hasn't the whole focus of this book been on how to work better, be more effective, make a bigger impact and be more successful? Well, yes, but that's not the whole picture. The secret to success is being satisfied in every part of your life, not just your work. Fulfilling, meaningful work that gives us a real buzz and a sense of satisfaction is an important part of our lives, but it's only that: a part. The chances are that the real fun, excitement and happiness in our lives come mainly from how we spend our time outside of work, and that's how it should be. If you spend all your time working, or thinking about work, you're missing out on everything else. It's not a good way to live.

That's why I want to encourage you to think about your life and lifestyle as a whole, and not just your work in isolation. Work is something that should add to, rather than detract from, the rest of your life. It's not your whole life, and it shouldn't be. Keep it in perspective.

REAL LIFE

My client Alan is a successful business consultant – so much so that his services are in enormous demand. He came to see me because he was working longer and longer hours and seeing less and less of his friends and family. He felt that his work–life balance was completely askew. We put together some simple action points to help him take control of his work life: leaving the office early twice a week, not responding to emails over the weekend, and so on. Alan now feels much happier, with more energy and enthusiasm for work when he is there – so his business is still booming!

IN A NUTSHELL

• Most work problems can be solved, and most mistakes can be rectified. Take the action you need to take, rather than spending time and energy on worry or regrets.

• Take the long-term view. If it's not going to matter in a day, a week, a month, it probably doesn't matter much now. Step back and retain your perspective.

• Your work is not your life. It may be an important part of your life, but it's not the whole picture. Never forget this.

If you'd like to learn more about keeping your perspective, I recommend: Cheryl Richardson, *Take Time for Your Life: A seven-step programme for creating the life you want*, Bantam Books, 2000.

A highly readable guide to taking control of your work and life. Full of exercises, real-life stories and recommendations for further resources.

34

Enjoy yourself!

You owe it to yourself to enjoy your work: you spend a lot of your time and energy there. If you really want to shine at work, you need to be motivated, engaged and passionate about what you do. Even if you really love your job, there are actions you can take to make work even more fun for you and other people.

Why you need to love what you do

The message of this chapter is very simple: enjoy yourself. If you want to shine at work, you absolutely have to be doing something that you enjoy. If you're not enjoying your job, you'll find it impossible to compete with the people around you who do! Think of some of the most successful business people you've heard or read about: what really seems to set them apart is their enthusiasm and excitement for what they do. Richard Branson is a great example – it's obvious from his infectious enthusiasm just how much he loves his work. But you don't have to be an entrepreneur to have that level of passion for your work: I believe that anyone can find work that they really love, where they can really shine.

More importantly, you owe it to yourself to enjoy your work because you spend so much of your time there! The average adult who works full-time will spend around 80,000 hours of their life at work. That's an eye-watering amount of time to spend doing something you don't enjoy.

Are you really happy at work?

You've pretty much reached the end of this book, so this is a good time to think about your job in its entirety. How much do you really enjoy your work? Let's look at some of the most common reasons for dissatisfaction at work – and what you can do about them if they apply to you.

- **You don't share the organisation's values**. Maybe you feel uncomfortable about the ethics of the company, or perhaps the culture is very driven and competitive, whereas you would prefer a more collaborative, team-oriented approach. If you feel that your personal values and approach are significantly at odds with those of your workplace, there's not a great deal that you can do to fix this: the organisation is bigger than you! Your only real option here is to move on.

- **You don't enjoy your day-to-day role**. If your role is very administrative, for example, but you would prefer to spend your time working face-to-face with clients, you're going to find it hard to stay motivated and enthusiastic. Go back to the early chapters in this book about your skills, strengths and personal brand. What do you have to offer, and are there ways in which you can incorporate more of what you enjoy into your role? Could you move sideways into another position that suits you better? If you've explored all the options, and still can't find a way of making your work more interesting and fun then, again, it's probably time to move on.

- **You don't have anything in common with your colleagues**. No one is saying that you have to be best friends with the people you work with, but the fact is that we derive a lot of our enjoyment of work from how we interact with the people around us. If your colleagues are unfriendly, unsociable, or simply not 'your kind of people', think seriously about your future in the organisation. Maybe it's a short-term issue, and when you move on to another role, the environment will be different. But look at the senior people in the organisation: if you feel that you can't identify with them in any way, it's going to be hard for you to make an impression. And you're unlikely to feel too happy. So maybe this isn't where your best future lies.

- **You enjoy your job, but not the things that come with it**. Perhaps you have a very long commute that drains you, or you routinely have to work long hours and/or weekends. Maybe you feel that you're not being paid enough for the amount of work that you do and the level of responsibility that you have. However much you enjoy the tasks you do on a day-to-day basis, issues like these can take away a lot of the pleasure from your work. The good news is that often they're fixable. Can you move closer to work? Would being a bit more organised and self-disciplined help you to avoid routinely long hours? Can you talk to your boss about a pay rise? Again, however, if there are 'peripheral' factors like these that are taking away your enjoyment of your work, and you can't find a way of solving them, it's time to think about moving on.

MAKING IT WORK IN PRACTICE

Rating your enjoyment

How would you rate your work on a scale of 1 to 10, where 1 is 'hate it' and 10 is 'love it'? If you're scoring less than 7 out of 10, you need to give this a bit more thought. Set aside half an hour and write down everything that you do enjoy about your work, and everything that you don't. How balanced is your list? What can you do to improve your overall enjoyment levels? Be honest with yourself: if you can't find ways of eliminating or at least minimising the aspects of work that you don't enjoy, it's time to think about making your next move.

Enjoy yourself now

Whether you're pretty happy with your job, or whether you've come to the conclusion that you need to move on in order to find the perfect role for you, make the effort to enjoy yourself in little ways. Even if you love your job, there are ways to increase your enjoyment at work further. And, if you've realised that you don't really enjoy your work and you're planning a job move, that's probably going to take a bit of time to achieve, so what can you do to make things better in the meantime? Here are some easy ways to make work more fun.

- **Smile**. Even something as simple as a smile or a cheerful 'good morning' can lift your spirits and those of the people you meet. It costs nothing, it makes you feel better, and it can make someone else's day.

- **Make friends**. Even if your colleagues aren't very sociable, you can still find ways of engaging them in conversation. Research has shown that chat and 'banter' in the office are one of the things that really help to energise people at work and make them feel involved. Of course you can't spend all day at the water cooler, but a little bit of chit-chat peppered through your day can help you to feel more involved, and can help to put your work in context: there is a life outside of work!

- **Treat yourself**. Make an effort to do one nice thing for yourself every day. That might be a cappuccino on the way into the office, or a walk in the park at lunchtime, or meeting a friend for a drink after work. Building little treats into your day will lift your spirits and give you something – however small – to look forward to.

- **Treat other people kindly**. Lots of self-help manuals advise that you commit an 'act of kindness' every day. It may sound a bit cheesy, but you will be amazed how good you feel when you do something nice for another person! It doesn't have to be a grand gesture: it could be something as simple as holding the lift for someone, or making your colleague a

REAL LIFE

My friend David used to work in a job that he really hated. Eventually, he woke up to the fact that he needed to move on, and found a new position that suited him much better. However, his employer insisted that he work his three months' notice and he was dreading that. He made the situation more tolerable by giving himself something specific to look forward to on a Monday evening. Because Monday was the day he hated most, Monday night became 'date night' – he and his girlfriend would go to the cinema, or out for drinks and dinner, or meet up with other friends. Having something fun to look forward to on a Monday made the beginning of each week more bearable.

cup of tea, or bringing chocolates into the office. Little acts of kindness like this can really brighten up your day – and, of course, they make you a nice person to be around!

The bottom line, as I've said before, is that life is too short for you to be stuck in a job that you don't really enjoy. You owe it to yourself to do work that is meaningful to you, that plays to your strengths, and that you feel engaged in. Anything less than this, and you're never going to be able to shine.

IN A NUTSHELL

• Life is too short to do something that you don't enjoy.

• Be honest about what you do and don't enjoy about your work. If the problem can't be fixed – move on.

• Take the time to enjoy yourself in little ways. Regular treats and small acts of kindness towards others will make your working day that much more enjoyable.

If you'd like to learn more about enjoying yourself at work, I recommend:
Sophie Rowan, *Happy at Work: Ten steps to ultimate job satisfaction*, Pearson Education Ltd, 2008.

Covers a range of topics including how to manage yourself, your colleagues and your working environment. Lots of practical examples and case studies make this an easy read.

A final word

I hope that you've found the ideas and suggestions in this book helpful, whether you're just starting out on your career, looking for your next move, simply trying to find ways to make your existing role more fulfilling or looking to claim back your work–life balance. Your career is a journey: you may have a bumpy ride now and again, and you might take the odd wrong turn but, ultimately, it's you who is in the driving seat. I hope very much that this book has encouraged you to take more control over your work – and to make it a fulfilling and fun part of your life.

The *Shine* library

David Allen, *Getting Things Done: How to achieve stress-free productivity*, Piatkus Books, 2002.
A comprehensive guide to helping you get in control of your workload once and for all.

Leo Babauta, *The Power of Less: The 6 productivity principles that will change your life*, Hay House UK Ltd, 2009.
A clear and concise guide to achieving more by doing less, including through setting limits on your commitments.

Duncan Bannatyne, *How To Be Smart With Your Time*, Orion Books, 2010.
A highly readable time-management guide from the star of *Dragons' Den*.

Edward de Bono, *Teach Yourself to Think*, Penguin, 1996.
This is the 'bible' of books on thinking, with a particular slant towards problem-solving. Highly recommended.

James Borg, *Persuasion: The art of influencing people*, Pearson Education Ltd, 2004.
A straightforward, easy and highly practical read, enhanced with lots of humorous examples.

Gillian Butler and Tony Hope, *Manage your Mind: The mental fitness guide*, Oxford University Press, 1995.
Down-to-earth advice on coping with stress and anxiety.

David Clutterbuck, *Everyone Needs a Mentor: Fostering talent in your organisation*, Chartered Institute of Personnel and Development, 2004.
The classic textbook on mentoring from one of the industry's experts. Geared more towards how to set up a mentoring scheme in your organisation, but lots of useful information on how to make a mentoring relationship work.

Stephen R. Covey, *The 7 Habits of Highly Effective People*, Simon & Schuster Ltd, 2004.
The 'bible' for business and personal planning. The writing style is a little dense and anecdote-heavy, but well worth persevering with.

Bill Ford, *High Energy Habits*, Simon & Schuster Ltd, 2002.
An extremely practical (and often very funny) guide to raising your energy by managing your work and home environment.

Michael Fullan, *The Six Secrets of Change: What the best leaders do to help their organizations thrive and survive*, Jossey Bass, 2008.
A fascinating study of change in the workplace. The writing style is quite 'academic', but worth persevering with!

Marshall Goldsmith, *What Got You Here Won't Get You There*, Profile Books Ltd, 2008.
A superb analysis of the attitudes and behaviours that hold us back in the workplace. Very highly recommended.

Richard Hall, *Brilliant Presentation: What the best presenters know, do and say*, Pearson Education Ltd, 2008.
A clear and simple guide to presenting to both large and small audiences.

Robert Holden, *Success Intelligence: Timeless wisdom for a manic society*, Hodder and Stoughton, 2005.
An in-depth but very readable guide to defining what success means for you, and how to achieve it through work.

Ros Jay, *How to Manage Your Boss: Or colleagues, or anybody else you need to develop a good and profitable relationship with*, Prentice Hall, 2002.
Don't be put off by the long title! This is a practical and very hands-on guide to managing other people, with the emphasis on how to manage your boss.

John Leach, *The Success Factor: Master the secret of a winning mindset*, Crimson Publishing, 2010.
A great book to dip in and out of, full of ideas for how to challenge yourself and your thinking to achieve success.

Judith Leary-Joyce, *The Psychology of Success: Secrets of serial achievement*, Pearson Education Ltd, 2009.
Thought-provoking material on identifying your values and needs in a work context

Nic Peeling, *Brilliant Manager: What the best managers know, do and say*, Pearson Education Ltd, 2008.
A practical and honest guide to handling the challenges that most managers face.

Tom Peters, *The Brand You 50: Fifty ways to transform yourself from an 'employee' into a brand that shouts distinction, commitment and passion!*, Alfred A. Knopf, 2000.
Although a decade old, this classic publication from the guru of branding is still as relevant – and inspiring – as ever.

Steve Radcliffe, *Leadership: Plain and simple*, Financial Times/Prentice Hall, 2009.
A brilliant and straightforward guide to the skills of leadership. Practical, direct and accessible.

Cheryl Richardson, *Take Time for Your Life: A seven-step programme for creating the life you want*, Bantam Books, 2000.
A highly readable guide to taking control of your work and life. Full of exercises, real-life stories and recommendations for further resources.

Stephen P Robbins, *The Truth About Managing People*, Pearson Education Ltd, 2008.
A comprehensive guide to managing behaviour in the workplace. As useful for team members as for managers.

Sophie Rowan, *Happy at Work: Ten steps to ultimate job satisfaction*, Pearson Education Ltd, 2008.
Covers a range of topics including how to manage yourself, your colleagues and your working environment. Lots of practical examples and case studies make this an easy read.

Martin E P Seligman, *Authentic Happiness*, Nicholas Brealey Publishing, 2003.
Thought-provoking chapters on identifying your signature strengths and applying them at work.

Steps to Success, *Make Effective Decisions: How to weigh up the options and make the right choice*, A&C Black Publishers Ltd, 2007.
A short and straightforward book that sets out the best way to approach decisions, especially when under pressure.

Carole Stone, *Networking: The art of making friends*, Vermilion Press, 2001.
A light-hearted but practical guide by the 'queen' of networking. The emphasis is more on social than business networking, but plenty of great advice applicable to all networking situations.

Richard Templar, *The Rules of Work*, Pearson Education Ltd, 2010.
A good general guide to workplace behaviour, with a strong emphasis on managing office politics.

Amanda Vickers, Steve Bavister and Jackie Smith, *Personal Impact: What it takes to make a difference*, Pearson Education Ltd, 2009.
A very practical guide to raising your profile and increasing your personal impact. Lots of exercises and case studies to illustrate the points being made.

Nick Williams, *The Work we Were Born to Do*, Element, 2009.
A thoughtful guide to discovering your work motivations and planning your career.

Jurgen Wolff, *Focus: The power of targeted thinking*, Pearson Education Ltd, 2008.
A practical guide to identifying and focusing on your goals and managing your time.

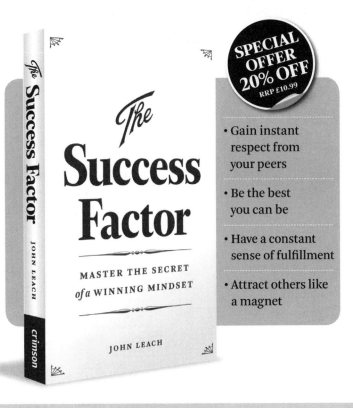

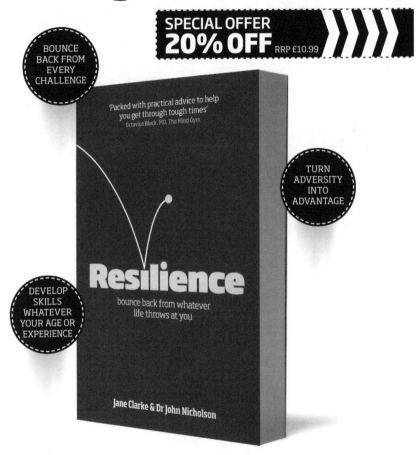